FOLLOWING BREEZE

A NAUTICAL NOVEL

BY

ED ROBINSON

This is dedicated to those intrepid souls who live on boats. Thanks to all the friends, acquaintances, and characters that cross our path, as we travel aboard Leap of Faith. You enrich our lives. I especially want to thank the cruising community in Marathon, Florida. This book was written in Boot Key Harbor, nestled in with hundreds of our closest friends, (Winter 2014/2015).

Prelude

The name's Breeze, Meade Edwin Breeze to be exact. Everyone has called me Breeze since high school. I am a man who once lived the American dream. I lost it all.

I bought an old trawler and retreated to remote parts of Florida to hide from society. I ended up growing dope on one island, and brewing rum on another, just to survive. I was on the run from the law, eating out of cans when I could afford to eat at all.

Eventually the Gods smiled upon me. and I had it all again. I bought a fancy new boat. I came to terms with the death of my wife. I traveled the Caribbean with a beautiful woman. Apparently, I couldn't stand prosperity, because I lost it all again. I'm back to running home-grown dope and eating out of cans, waiting for that new boat to be sold.

Until then, I was still trawler trash.

Ashes Aweigh

"What do you mean you sent the money to Miss Mongeon?" I screamed into the phone. The Miami broker who had been trying to sell my late model Grand Banks trawler, had just informed me that it had indeed finally been sold. Six hundred grand had been wired to the account of my twice-ex lover Andi Mongeon. I was livid. The boat was mine and it was my last hope for survival.

"I'm sorry, Mr. Breeze," said Dano the broker. "We simply wired the proceeds to the person named on the title as owner. It was Miss Mongeon who paid for the original purchase. She signed the paperwork."

That much was true. I was so far on the wrong side of the law that I couldn't put it in my name. The money I was awarded in my wife's wrongful death lawsuit had been deposited into Andi's account. She had written the check and filled out the paperwork, but that boat was mine.

"I believe I'll make my way to Miami and tear you a new asshole, asshole," I spit into the receiver. "Tell your pervert boss I'm coming for him too. You both knew that was my boat."

"Now calm down Mr. Breeze," stuttered Dano. "There is no need to blame us. This is between you and Miss Mongeon. If the vessel truly belonged to you, there should be no problems. We can't get involved in personal affairs."

Trouble was, I had no idea where she went. She was gone, along with most of my money. This was a mortal blow to my prospects. This whole deal stunk. There had to be a way to recover what was rightfully mine. I tried to think quickly, come up with an angle.

"Let me ask you a question, you blue-blazer wearing piece of shit," I said. "Do you remember who signed the contract for you to broker the sale of *Ashes Aweigh*? It wasn't Miss Mongeon. She never gave you permission to sell. She didn't authorize shit. I think a decent lawyer would have something to work with there. I was the one who signed off on the sale. If I didn't own it, then that contract is worthless. Would you agree?"

The phone was muffled, like he had his hand over the receiver. A long pause was followed by hesitant words. "I can't say how that might work Mr. Breeze," said Dano. "We feel as if we followed the spirit of the law by selling the yacht and transferring the money to its legal owner."

"I'm talking about the letter of the law," I replied. "I think you may end up sorry for screwing me."

I had no clue what I was talking about or how the law might apply. I couldn't risk taking legal action or the law would find me. I had to stay far away from the law, or go to jail. The technicality may have ruffled Dano's feathers a bit though. He could get into trouble maybe, lose his license or something. I suppose that was better than me breaking his neck.

"You haven't heard the last from me, you son of a bitch," I yelled. "Sleep with one eye open."

With that I hung up. Let the bastard sweat. I had no intention of going to Miami. Hell, I couldn't afford to get there. *Think Breeze, think.* I'd spent almost a year dreaming of the day when I'd get that money. It had sustained me. I'd been kicked in the balls plenty of times over those past few years, but this one hurt the most. It took away my hope.

I was sitting at the nav station aboard *Leap of Faith*, with my head in my hands, trying to cope. The shock to my brain was preventing me from thinking clearly. I took a couple deep breaths and tried to control my rage. I was good and screwed this time, but what to do? This situation was so unjust, even a loser like me should be able to figure something out. As I calmed myself, no solutions came. I dug into the old coffee can and grabbed a few twenties. Maybe a few cold beers at the Tiki Bar would clear my head. Although the tactic of getting drunk had never solved my problems in the past, I was willing to keep trying. What else did I have?

I locked my dinghy up to the dock and walked under the Matanzas Bridge until it came to a dead-end. I hung a left, passed through an opening in the fence, and entered the Tiki Bar from the back. I looked around for friendly faces until I saw Robin, Diver Dan, and one-legged Beth sitting at a table by the pool. They all lived aboard boats in the harbor at Fort Myers Beach. We'd become friends when I could no longer afford a mooring ball and started anchoring in the river with the other poor folk.

Diver Dan, who didn't dive anymore, was the ringleader. He had rescued Beth from homelessness and put her up in her own boat. I never got the gist of their relationship, and I didn't ask. Her prosthetic was nothing more than a manikin leg. She attached it with neoprene elbows and knees cut from thrift shop wet suits. Robin was the actual diver. He was a nice guy, with a bright intelligence that you didn't often encounter in the near homeless. Dan drummed up the business and collected the cash. Robin cleaned boat bottoms and did other odd jobs. I'm not sure how one-legged Beth contributed, other than to keep them both happy. She was a free spirited maverick who bounced from manic to depressive like she was on a pogo stick. She actually wasn't bad looking, in a trailer park sort of way, especially when she had her teeth in. She might be wearing a ratty tee shirt with no bra, and no teeth one day. The next day she would be wearing a cute little sundress, have her hair brushed nicely, and be somewhat sober. I liked her either way. I was in no position to judge. I wasn't exactly overrun with friends either.

Diver Dan had been sharing his wisdom garnered through his thirty years of life aboard. He explained his philosophy of taking his retirement in installments. He worked when he had to, and relaxed once he raised enough dough to kick back. I liked his attitude towards life, so we had hit it off. He knew I was broke, and probably suspected that I was running from something, but he didn't pry. When we swapped stories, Robin would mostly just listen, while Beth would wander off to flirt with whoever would tolerate her.

"It's a dog-eat-dog world, Dan," I complained. "And I'm wearing a milk bone necklace."

What's got you bitching, Breeze," answered Dan. "Doesn't sound like you."

I vaguely explained that I'd been screwed out of a large sum of money, and wasn't sure what to do about it. He gave me a skeptical look. He didn't know all the facts concerning my pot farming or how I survived.

"Legal money?" he asked.

"Yup, it should have been all legit," I said. "But a legal technicality is keeping it out of my hands."

Dan pointed his beer bottle at one of the televisions behind the bar. Yet another Morgan and Morgan commercial played. The head ambulance chaser was advising you that you may have been harmed by some drug or another.

"You need a good lawyer," offered Dan. "Legal technicalities call for lawyers."

That's when it hit me. I needed to talk with Mike Savage, the lawyer who had handled the wrongful death case for me. It had made him a million dollars. He owed me. I had squandered my three million, most of it anyway. Andi ran off with the rest. The sale of *Ashes Aweigh* was supposed to be my salvation.

"Sorry to bolt folks," I said, after I downed the last of my beer. "I've got to run. I suddenly have some business to take care of."

Savage Law

Mike Savage had been a lawyer down on his luck. Cases were few and far between, and his firm was on the verge of bankruptcy. I had originally refused to settle out of court, but eventually I was so desperate for money that I accepted an offer. Mike had pocketed a cool million as a result. I understood that his firm had made a nice comeback. The way I saw it, he owed me a favor. I knew he couldn't handle a Florida case for me, but I could certainly use some advice. Maybe he had legal associates that could help. I was once again desperate. I had nothing to lose by asking.

I explained the situation, emphasizing the fact that I had signed the sales contract with the broker. If Andi was technically the owner, she had not agreed to the contract.

"I don't know Breeze," said Mike. "It feels like there ought to be something we can do, but it's a bit thin. This is not my area of expertise."

"I know, Mike," I answered. "But I've got nowhere else to turn. Please look into this for me. Send a fancy lawyer letter to those assholes and threaten them. Buy me some time."

"You've got to find the girl, Breeze," replied Mike. "Get the money directly from her. Make a deal. Threaten her. Charm her. She's your ticket."

"I've got no clue where she is, Mike," I said. "She could be anywhere in the world."

There was a long silence. Finally, Mike spoke.

"You know I used to be a cop, right, Breeze?"

I remembered that.

"I still have connections. I have friends that are expert skip-tracers. I use them to collect debts sometimes. If anyone can find her, they can."

"Okay, Mike," I said. "But don't drop the legal angle. Talk to someone that deals in contract law. Promise you'll pursue this."

"All right, Breeze," he said. "It's the least I can do. Don't get too excited until you hear from me. I'll let you know when or if I get a better handle on this."

I thanked him and hung up the phone. What would I do if Mike's friends located her? I couldn't hitchhike to Timbuktu, or wherever she had gone. I needed money. I needed more money than one dope run would bring. I almost laughed at the irony of my circumstances. I could be somewhat wealthy, if I could only raise enough money to go get it. *Another fine mess you've gotten yourself into Breeze.*

That night I sat alone on the boat, swatting mosquitoes and pondering how dismal my life had become. I couldn't blame bad luck. Other than my wife's death, it had all been my fault. Losing her had triggered an endless series of bad decisions.

I embezzled from my employer. I left everything behind and ran away from life. I bought an old boat and hid out in the mangroves of southwest Florida. I lurked on the edges of society, dealing with vagrants and other dropouts. The dope that I grew on the island of Cayo Costa earned me just enough to eat and keep the boat afloat.

It was a bare-bones existence, but it kept me away from the law. They had tried to find me, either for theft or tax evasion, but I had stayed one step ahead of them. The feeling that it couldn't last forever was ever-present. One day I'd slip up.

I had almost turned things around the previous year. Just when I was at my lowest, talking to my wife's ashes and about to give up, an angel intervened. My college girlfriend found me in a bar in Fort Myers Beach. I got the settlement check, and together we traveled the Caribbean aboard *Ashes Aweigh*. I completed my life's mission to spread Laura's ashes in the BVI. Andi completed her mission to rescue me from despair, and then she left.

She left me with enough money to make it back to the states and pay for the total refurbishing of my trusty trawler, *Leap of Faith*. I put *Ashes Aweigh* up for sale and went about my life. She had freed me from my prison of grief, but I was still alone. Where she went I couldn't guess. I looked for her in Fort Myers Beach with no luck. Now my new mission in life would be to find her. I had to find her and convince her that the money was mine.

Two days later I got a call from Mike Savage. His people had come through.

"She used her passport in Puerto Plata, Dominican Republic," he told me. "That was months ago. No other activity on her passport after that."

"She's in Luperon," I said. "We stayed there together for a long time. She loved it there."

"Well, there you have it," said Mike. "Your weak legal angle is just that, by the way, weak. You've got to go and talk to her."

Son of a bitch! How the hell was I going to get to the Dominican? It was a long way off for *Leap of Faith*, and I couldn't simply hop a plane and fly down there. I had learned the hard way about using my own passport. The Man had almost caught up with me in Mayaguana. I was red-flagged with the State Department.

I needed cash. The only way to start was to sell my dope. I had a fresh batch that needed to be shipped down to Marathon. Maybe my old friend Tiki Terry would have some ideas. It would be nice to get back down there and have a cold one at the Dockside. On my last trip I had gotten fond of a new waitress there named Lisa. She lived on her sailboat Amigo, out in Boot Key Harbor. A trip to Marathon was just what I needed. It was a place to start at least.

For the past year I had been making monthly runs from Cayo Costa to Marathon to sell my pot. I called this endeavor, Operation Island Smile. I grew it on an island and it made folks smile. The previous year, I had taken *Ashes Aweigh* all through the Bahamas, the Turks and Caicos, the Dominican Republic, Puerto Rico and the British Virgin Islands. Andi and I lived like royalty.

We also spent like royalty, burning through my cash at an incredible rate. It was a year to remember. We shared a lifetime of experiences in a tropical paradise. I pulled out of my funk and regained my old self. I was able to overcome my grief and move on in life. I still had a small part of Laura's ashes, but I rarely spoke to them anymore.

It was foolish to blow all my cash on that boat and the trip, but I had no regrets. Except now, Andi had my future in her bank account, apparently. Did she do it on purpose? Could she be that cold? I couldn't believe that she might be capable of stealing from me, again. I didn't begrudge her the money she took from me when she left. She had saved my very soul, after all. What would I do if the money was hers, and the broker sent it all to me? Would I keep it? Maybe so, it's hard to say. I had to talk to her somehow.

Making Deals in Marathon

I said my goodbyes to my three amigos; Robin, Diver Dan, and one-legged Beth. I pulled up anchor, and idled thru the bay. Once I had steered *Leap of Faith* under the Matanzas Bridge and around Bowditch Point, I throttled up to cruising speed and pointed her south. Other than the occasional field of stone crab pots, there were no obstacles between Fort Myers Beach and Boot Key Harbor. I could make the trip in less than twenty hours without pushing it. *Leap of Faith* had undergone a total restoration while I was in the Caribbean. That's where the last of my money went. Howie and his crew at Marathon Boat Yard did an outstanding job. *Miss Leap* was now the finest vessel of her class anywhere in the world, at least in my opinion. I was proud of her. She was ready to travel. She was also the only thing between me and homelessness.

I engaged the auto-pilot and sat back to watch the blue sea go by. My thoughts returned to Andi and the money. I had come to terms with the prospect of never seeing her again. As beautiful and smart as she was, I had not truly loved her. I had loved Laura with my entire being. I loved my old boat. Something was missing between me and Andi though. I never figured it out. Around her I was always a bit intimidated. I could never feel completely comfortable in her presence. She was stunning and desirable. I did enjoy being with her, but we just didn't share the complete intimacy that I once had with Laura.

After the first hour, I made all my systems checks and decided everything was kosher. I pushed Andi out of my mind and started to contemplate my upcoming business deal. Tiki Terry was the only person I dealt with in Marathon. It was easy. I delivered a pound or two of dope, and he paid cash. He took care of the distribution on his end. I make enough to survive for another month. I never tried to expand my operation for fear of being caught. I knew there were warrants for my arrest. Getting busted on a marijuana charge would lead to worse charges resurfacing.

I needed to get Terry to talk in private about making some kind of bigger score. He knew everyone in the Keys. Nothing happened between Key West and Key Largo that he didn't know about. What better place to try to hit it big? Drugs were rampant, as were scams. I was desperate enough to run either.

Finally, I passed under the Seven Mile Bridge, gateway to the lower Keys. I turned *Leap of Faith* to port and cut across to Boot Key. I hailed Dockside on the radio to ask about water depths out in front of their place. Boot Key Harbor is carpeted with mooring balls, which I couldn't afford. There were very limited places to anchor, which is free. I remembered seeing some free space directly out from Dockside on my last visit, but didn't see any deep draft vessels there. One of the boaters at Dockside returned my call.

"Yea *Leap of Faith.* You got as little as four foot of water at dead-low tide, but most of the time there's five or six feet there," he informed me.

That meant that I'd be sitting on the bottom occasionally, but it would have to do. At least it would be a short dinghy ride to the bar.

I called Tiki Terry to let him know I was in town.

"When can we meet for a beer?" I asked. That was code for "I've got the dope." I didn't have to tell him to meet at Dockside. That was understood.

"Glad to hear from you, Breeze," Terry said. "Been waiting on you. Tomorrow night good?"

I told him that was fine. I'd get a chance to check on boat systems after the trip. Maybe I'd see if Lisa was working.

Terry and I made our deal the next night. After a few beers with the gang, I pulled him aside.

"Can I talk to you in private?" I asked.

"Sure man, what's up?" he said.

"I've got a situation," I started. "I need to make a big score, but I don't know how. I figured you'd be the one to ask. Got any idea how I can cash in big. Just a one shot deal?"

"You in trouble, Breeze?" asked Terry.

I explained the whole thing to him. I told him about the boat, about the money and about Andi being in Luperon. I hoped she was in Luperon anyway. Terry had been good to me, friendly even. He was the only person I could trust.

"Let's go back inside and get another beer," he said. "Let me think for a minute."

Back inside we went. We got our drinks and sat down away from the crowd. Terry started pealing the label off his bottle and shaking his head. He appeared to be arguing with himself. After a few minutes he looked me in the eye.

"You think long and hard about what I'm about to tell you," he said. "No one else can know. I'm going to give you a name, and you're on your own after that."

"Shoot," I said.

"Bald Mark," was his reply. "Lives on his boat up in Tavernier."

"And what does this Bald Mark do?" I asked.

"He runs coke," Terry said. "Lots of it. He's got guys in fast boats that run offshore and pick it up from trawlers. He's also got the cops in his pocket. He used to be a cop himself. He knows when it's safe to make a run."

"You think he can use me somehow?" I asked.

"Don't know," said Terry. "That part is up to you. I'm good with Bald Mark, but he's a bad man. That's my warning to you. He takes care of his people, but those that cross him end up with broken bones, or dead."

"I don't know," I said. "Sounds like a rough character. I'm not exactly a gangster."

"You want to make a score?" Terry said. "He's the fastest way I know of down here. He'll decide if you are worth a shot. Drop my name, but not so anyone else can hear. You got it?"

"I got it. Where can I find this guy?"

"Blue Waters Marina, on the Hawk Channel side. Up by the Triangles, marker 39. Pick up a winding channel that goes all through a bunch of houses and condos and shit. You'll think you're lost, but it opens up once you get inside. First is Curtis Marine, then Blue Waters. It's quiet and secluded. Bald Mark holds court under the tiki hut every afternoon."

"Thanks Terry," I said. "I'm nervous about this, but I'm going to go talk to him."

"Good luck, Breeze," he said. "Watch your back. Don't cross him in anyway. I hope you get your money from that woman. Now beat it. I'll get the check."

I went back to the boat and plopped down in a deck chair. Here I was again. I hitched a ride on life and it keeps dropping me off at crossroads, with no directions. *Working for a coke kingpin? Really Breeze?* I knew it was a stupid move. I was going to do it anyway. That had been the story of my life since Laura died.

I went inside the salon and picked up the film canister that held what was left of her ashes. I had spread the rest on the beach at Norman Island. I needed to do that, but I couldn't bring myself to let go of her completely. I kept a little part of her with me. I put the canister on the table in front of me and spoke to it.

"What do you think Laura? I've got to get to Andi and get my money. Sorry about her, by the way. I know it's wrong. What else can I do?"

The canister refused to answer. It just sat there, unmoving, feeling sorry for me. Not because of my dire circumstance, but because I was stupid enough to throw in with a cocaine dealer. I picked it up and carried it outside to watch the sun set. I hadn't done that in a long time. It made me nostalgic. It also made me miss my wife deeply. This was as good a time as any for a grown man to cry, but I choked it back. I would need to be tough to deal with Bald Mark.

Bald Mark

Getting in to Blue Waters Marina was just as Terry described. There was no place to anchor in the basin that I could tell, so I called the marina on the radio. They told me they were full, and could not accept transients. They did, however, have a spot on the T-head if I wanted to come in for lunch. I said that would be fine. I had come forty-two miles in just over six hours, and was ready for a beer.

Leap of Faith is called a thirty-six footer, but she's really thirty-nine feet overall. The spot they directed me to looked to be about forty feet long. It was between two expensive looking yachts. Their stainless steel anchors glistened liked polished silver, threatening to stab *Miss Leap*, if I screwed up. I was damn good with her though, so I didn't hesitate. I poked her bow towards the middle of the open slot, approaching like I was about to ram the dock. At the precise time necessary, I brought the wheel over hard to port, and goosed the throttle just a bit to start her spinning. I spun the wheel back hard to starboard and dropped her in reverse. Another goose of the throttle to stop her forward momentum, and she drifted right into place. As we floated up to the dock, kissing the pilings ever so gently, I climbed down from the helm and tossed a bow line onto the dock. I hopped over the gunnel with a stern line, wrapped it around a cleat, and then repeated the procedure at the bow. I had parallel parked a single-screw trawler slicker than snot.

Looking up the docks, I could make out the familiar thatched roof of a tiki hut. My tricky docking maneuver had boosted my confidence, so I walked right to it using a sure stride. Once I entered the shade of the bar, there was no doubt who was Bald Mark. The man wasn't just bald, he had no hair anywhere. He had no eyebrows, no arm pit hair, or hair on his chest. He was as smooth as a silk sheet. He wasn't very tall, maybe five-nine or so, but he was severely chiseled.

His muscles were so defined, that he appeared to be cut from stone. He was broad in the shoulders and thick in the chest. His eyes were black. I'd never seen anyone with black eyes. They deflated my confidence as he stared me down.

This was his turf, and I didn't belong. He was letting me know that I was on shaky ground, walking into his bar. Three Latinos sat at the adjacent table. All were wearing wife beater tee-shirts and sporting lots of bling. None was as cut as Bald Mark, but they were all tall and fit. The biggest of the three stood and nodded in my direction.

"You lost?" he asked.

"I'm here to see him," I said, nodding in Bald Mark's direction.

"Well, he's not accepting visitors today," the guy said. "Not today, not ever."

This wasn't going well. I hadn't known what to expect once I found Bald Mark, but I figured I'd at least get to talk to him. I stood up just a little taller, strengthened my resolve, and said, "I think he might talk to me." I looked Bald Mark right in the eyes, and bowed my head ever so slightly, trying to signal that I was no threat.

"Let him come," said Bald Mark.

The tall Latino, waved an arm toward Mark and let me pass. I walked over to Mark's table and sat across from him. I sat quietly for a full minute while Mark stared me down. Then he smiled.

"You've got balls," he said. "And I'm in a good mood today. Why are you here?"

"Job hunting," I said. "Terry Higgins sent me."

That caused him to raise an eyebrow, except he didn't really have any eyebrows. He stared me down some more, taking a drink of his beer. The creases of his biceps rippled as he raised the bottle. The dude was a freak, but his smile seemed genuine. With all those muscles and those black eyes, he radiated a fierce quality that made me nervous. The three amigos were all watching in silence. There was no music. I was tense, but Bald Mark seemed completely relaxed. Maybe I was his entertainment for the afternoon.

"What's your name, captain?" asked Bald Mark.

"They call me Breeze," I answered.

"Well Breeze, what type of qualifications do you possess, that may interest a man like me?"

"I can run a boat better than anyone in the Keys," I said. "That's no exaggeration. I'm damn good with boats."

"I saw you put that trawler in the hole down there. We all watched you come in," he said. "Impressive, but I've got enough boat men. Those three and a couple more."

I was stymied again. *Think Breeze.* I had to offer him something. He didn't seem like a man with a lot of patience.

"So how's it work?" I asked. "All five boats go out at once?"

"Yes," he said. "The shipments get split five ways. My boats all take off in different directions. If one of them gets caught, I still have eighty percent of the load."

"And you've got the cops looking the other way?"

"That's right," he said. "But that's only on land. Out on the water you've got the Coast Guard, DEA, and even the FWC to worry about. Go-fast boats in the Florida Straits draw a lot of attention."

That's when I came up with something. I made my pitch.

"So here's the deal," I said. "You see that classic trawler down there?"

"Fine looking vessel," he said.

"I run the whole load. I pick it up and walk right in, to any dock you want me to. She's much less conspicuous than a forty-foot Cigarette boat. No one would suspect a thing. Just a cruiser traveling the Keys. Plus I've got plenty of places to hide shit on board."

"I don't know," he said. "My way has worked pretty well so far."

"How much you pay these guys?" I asked.

"Each boat makes ten grand per run," he said.

"I'll do it for half. The whole load, one run, for twenty-five."

I had made my play. It was up to Bald Mark to decide now. I rose and walked over to the bar to get a beer. I deserved it. That first gulp went down cold and smooth. I hoped it wouldn't be my last. I walked back to his table, but didn't sit. I doubted he would invite me to sit and drink with him all afternoon. He slid a card across the table.

"Call me ten sharp tomorrow morning," he said. "I'll call Terry, check you out. Think it over."

"Thanks," was all I could say.

"Don't thank me yet," replied. "That number goes anywhere and you're dead. Those three won't like you cutting their pay either. Watch your back."

He fixed his black-eyed stare on me again. He was not smiling. I took my cue and walked out. One of the three stooges snarled at me as I passed. *What are you getting yourself into Breeze?*

I fired up *Leap of Faith* and studied my escape plan. Getting in was one thing, getting out was another. I was a little less cocky after my meeting with Bald Mark. I untied the lines, and used a boat hook to shove her bow away from the dock. While scrambling to the helm, I saw all of them standing at the rail, watching me. I gave the bow thruster a long burst and Miss Leap swung clear of the other boats. I bumped the throttle with the wheel hard to port and swung almost on a dime towards the fairway. I took one last look over my shoulder. Bald Mark was slowly clapping. The other three were standing stiff, with their arms crossed.

The winds were picking up out of the south as I entered Hawk Channel. I steered south and decided to go under the Channel Five Bridge and anchor for the night near Islamorada. I had fond memories of the time Andi and I ate and drank at the LoreLei. I had a few bucks from the dope deal with Tiki Terry. Dinner and drinks sounded good.

I called Bald Mark at precisely ten o'clock the next morning.

"Terry says you're trustworthy," he said. "Just trying to make a buck. He also says you are his dope dealer."

"That's right," I responded. "It's my only source of income."

"If you're running dope, why do you want to work with me?" asked Mark.

"Terry is my only customer," I responded. "Supply is limited. I barely make enough to survive."

"You find a bale floating offshore or something?" He asked.

Everybody asks me that question, I thought. I gave him my pat answer.

"Something like that," I said. I didn't want anyone to know that I was just growing a few plants, or where I was growing them.

"Pot is too bulky for my boats, and there's less profit margin," he said. "If I had your trawler in my fleet though, maybe it would be worth bringing in."

I just wanted to make one quick score. I didn't want to be a part of his fleet. I could see those black eyes staring me down in my mind. Before I could say anything, he started talking again.

"I've decided to give you an audition," he said. "You bring in the coke tomorrow night. If all goes well, we can talk about what you and your boat can do for me in the future. There will be no one-hit wonders in my outfit. Either you work for me or you don't."

This was bad. This was really bad. I could do the job and take off with my earnings, but I remembered what Terry had said about crossing Bald Mark. I had thrown in with the devil, and it was going to burn me. I thought about Andi down in Luperon. I had to get to her. I had made it my life's mission, just like I had with Laura's ashes. I had to agree to his terms. I'd figure out how to get out of the situation later. If I got my hands on the six hundred grand that was rightfully mine, I could run and hide forever.

"Well?" asked Mark. "You in, or are you out?"

"I'm in," I said. "Tell me what to do."

"Come see me so we can talk in person," he said. "Get here as soon as you can."

"On my way," I answered. "See you this afternoon."

Crap Breeze. You are one world class screw-up. I had once been a respectable businessman. I became a thief. I became a dope dealer. I became a boat bum. Now I was a coke-running gangster in the Florida Keys. I had just enlisted in the Bald Mark maritime militia. Where would it end? I had this idea, that if I got the money, I could somehow pull myself out of this mess.

I steered *Leap of Faith* back under the Channel Five Bridge and up to Tavernier. The T-head was open so no fancy piloting skills were needed. I was grateful. My nerves weren't up for it. I found him at the same table he was sitting at before. The three caballeros were not present. I got a beer from the bar and approached him. He told me to sit.

"Leave tonight for the Marquesas," he said. "Anchor off the southwest corner and wait. Tomorrow night just before midnight, start that tub and pull up anchor. Hover until you get a signal. "

"What's the signal?" I asked.

"Channel sixty-eight, near midnight, you will hear a series of clicks but no voice. The shrimper you're going to hook up with will be keying his mike repeatedly. That's the signal. He'll be running east to west in the West Channel, with his booms out. You always dock on your starboard side the way you did yesterday?"

"I prefer it," I said. "The helm is on the starboard side, easier to see."

"Okay, you'll approach the shrimper while under way, on his port, your starboard. He'll bring in his port boom to give you space. He'll slow down to three knots. Have some fenders out and come alongside. His crew will transfer five packages. Once clear, stow them good and return to the Marquesas. Leave the next morning for Stock Island Marina. I lined up a slip for you already. They know you're coming. One more thing, I'm giving each of my men a grand out of your pay to appease their hurt feelings. You get twenty."

"How do I get rid of the packages?" I asked. I didn't want to argue about my cut. Twenty thousand would get me to Luperon and back.

"My guys will come for them," he said. "By land. Don't leave the boat until they take custody. Understood?"

"Got it," I said.

My voiced sounded sure and strong, but on the inside I was nervous as hell. He was forcing me to make a tricky maneuver at sea, in the dark. The waters around the Marquesas and the Dry Tortugas were littered with ship wrecks. I had sold him on my skills as a boat operator though, so I couldn't chicken out now. He had called it an audition, after all.

"I'll be on station, waiting for the signal," I said. "Your packages will be safe with me."

"They better be," he said.

Coke in the Marquesas

Key West may be the end of the road, but it's not the end of the Keys. There are quite a few more islands stretching out to the west, terminating at the Dry Tortugas. These islands mark the separation of the Gulf of Mexico and the Atlantic Ocean. The waters are known for treacherous shoals, sand bars, and sunken treasure.

Leaving Key West by boat, I skirted the Kingfish Shoals below Crayfish Key and swung to the west. I passed Man Key, Woman Key and some mangrove islands with no name. I cruised on beyond Boca Grande Key, and in a few more miles approached the Marquesas Keys. I had never attempted to get in close to these islands. The water is shallow, and strewn with rocks. I didn't like it one bit. The weather was calm, and visibility was excellent. The water here was as clear and pretty as any in the Caribbean. I decided to drop anchor in seven foot of water between two marked wrecks. I was a mile due north of the markers designating Marquesas Rock and Cosgrove Shoal, just barely out of the channel. I didn't want to risk damaging *Miss Leap* by going in any further. Once I was sure the hook was set, I sat back and waited.

Midnight was approaching, so I fired up the engine. It sounded incredibly loud out here. The night had been totally silent. Millions of stars shone in the clear night sky. I made a bunch more noise pulling up the anchor. The chain rattling through the windlass startled me. My nerves were on edge. I cranked up the volume on the VHF radio, and tuned to channel sixty-eight. It was almost midnight when I heard the click, click, click of a mic being keyed. It was time to go.

I hadn't seen the shrimper, but suddenly it lit up like a small city. He had been running dark. He was indeed heading to the west, on a line that would bring us just south of the Quicksands, a really nasty shoal that had once been littered with Spanish gold. I hoped he wouldn't drift too far north while we made the transfer. He slowed as I neared. I could see crewmen working to bring in the nets. I watched the portside boom fold in. I heard one word over the radio. It was the Spanish word for hurry up.

Here we go Miss Leap. If anything goes wrong, I apologize in advance. The closer I got to the old shrimp boat, the more familiar it looked. Its steel hull was streaked with rust. Smoke poured out of the exhaust as if the engine needed some work. It slowed in the soft rolling sea as I pulled alongside. I made out the name painted on the bow. Dragon Fly, which was a boat I had seen often in Fort Myers Beach. The Fort Myers shrimp fleet ran from Florida to Texas and back. Key West had a smaller fleet that generally worked these waters. I wondered how many of them had delivered a payload like this one.

I didn't see anything that might go wrong. I had my fenders out, and the shrimper had old tires hanging off the side. The seas were calm. There was plenty of light. The captain of the other boat was waving me in.

I angled closer, timing the swells. Four crewmen stood by, next to something under a tarp. We bumped together briefly, and then we separated. I could hear men shouting. We came together again and they made lines fast to my boat. The captain pointed straight ahead a couple times, telling me to just keep going straight. I could hear and feel men coming aboard. I just held her steady. This was no time to investigate. They were just loading packages.

I watched as three of the crew returned to the shrimper and let loose the lines. Where was the fourth? The captain waved me away. I veered off and began a slow sweeping turn back to the east. His lights went out. It was done. I made sure we were in the center of the channel and set a course back to the Marquesas. I hit the autopilot and went below to have a look. There stood one of Bald Mark's men. It was the tall one who had snarled at me. He lifted his shirt to show me the pistol stuffed in his waistband, and smiled. The dude did have nice teeth.

"El Jefe sent me to keep an eye on you, and his delivery," he said. "Nice night for a boat ride."

"Welcome aboard," I said. "I could have handled this by myself."

"We are not so sure we can trust you," he said. "At least not yet. Senor Mark did not get wealthy by being stupid. I assure you."

"I just want a payday," was my reply. "I need to get back to the wheel. Make yourself comfortable."

I climbed the ladder to the bridge and he followed. We didn't speak again until we were safely anchored off the Marquesas. We stowed the goods in the hold. I didn't use the compartments down there for anything. The tightly wrapped bundles fit nicely. I covered the hatches with crates of canned goods and some old ropes.

"You might work out, and you might not," said the Latino. "My name is Enrique, but you can call me Rick. Do not call me Ricky. If and when you fuck up, I will be the one to punish you."

"Like I said, I just want a pay day. I'm not trying to shake things up or step on your toes."

"If you decide otherwise, we will have it out, man to man," He said.

He was bigger than me. He was stronger, younger and probably no stranger to violence. I had been an athlete in my day, but those days were long gone. I wanted no part of a fight with him. I cringed at the thought of him coming after me once I crossed Bald Mark. I'd cross that bridge when I came to it.

I tried to sleep, but my thoughts made it difficult. The once Great and Mighty Breeze had sunken to yet another new low. I had fouled *Miss Leap's* bilge with evil. I had held hands with evil-doers. I had sold my soul and infected my vessel. I was worse than trawler trash. I was scum.

I tried to convince myself once again, that it would all work out. Get the money from Andi. Make a new life someplace. Go where they can't find you and leave it all behind. Hell, that's how I got in this mess in the first place. I tried to run away. I tried to leave it all behind. *How'd that work out for ya, Breeze?* I thought briefly how I might use the money to set things straight.

I could go legit. Pay my dues. That thought didn't last long. *Just get the money, Breeze. First things first.*

I had never been to Stock Island, but the approach was simple enough. Stock Island sits between Key West and Boca Chica Key. The channel is well marked. I got my slip assignment and we docked without a hitch. My new friend, Rick, was quick with the lines. He didn't look like a boater, but I supposed his time running go-fast boats for Bald Mark had taught him a thing or two. He made a quick call as soon as we got settled.

"Done, we are at the marina," was all he said before hanging up.

"The guys will bring duffels. They will have a few drinks, come and go from your boat a few times. After dark, the stuff gets offloaded. The marina staff will look the other way. Everything goes smooth, you get your cut."

Everything went smooth. I got my cut. I added a nice, clean stack of crisp one-hundred dollar bills to the coffee can. It eased my conscience considerably. I decided to make use of the on-sight bar. I guzzled the first beer, then I asked for another. The nice barmaid kept them coming after that. When Bald Mark sat down beside me, I was nice and loose.

"I didn't need a babysitter," I said.

"I like to keep eyes on my investments," he answered. "Rick says you did just fine. He doesn't like you much, but he's impressed with your boat handling skills. I am too."

"Thanks for the kind words," I said.

"It's going to take some time to clear today's haul through the system," he said. "Take some time off, spend some of that money."

"So where's the stuff come in from?" I asked. "I'd think the law would be on to shrimpers coming from South America these days."

"Comes up from Cuba," he said. "The Cubans take all the risk getting it that far. We only have to make it ninety miles."

I found that hard to believe. President Obama had made some overtures about normalizing relations with

Cuba recently, but getting cocaine out of that country seemed improbable.

"How the hell does that work?" I asked.

"I've got a good friend," he said. "General Leopoldo Cintra Frias. He is the Minister of the whole damned Revolutionary Armed Forces. He took over three years ago when Julio Reguiro died. He used to be Deputy Minister, good commie. Pals around with Raul Castro."

"How does one becomes friends with the head of the Cuban army?" I asked.

"Human trafficking," he said. "I've brought several of his relatives to the states safely. He pays me well. He trusts me. He's a good commie, because he is wealthy by Cuban standards. Some of his relatives are not so fortunate. Some get on Raul's wrong side, so they escape certain imprisonment, or even death."

I thought that over for a minute. Bald Mark had some kind of relationship with a big cheese in Cuba. He rescued his relatives or friends or whatever. It was pretty deep stuff. Go fast boats would come in handy for that sort of thing. Political connections would too. It had to be very expensive for a high profile refugee to get a free pass to America.

"So, do you sit and have drinks with this guy or what?" I asked.

"I have, but not lately. Since Obama's overtures to Raul, everything is crazy down there. Frias knows that nothing will benefit the people of Cuba. Only the Castros, and people like Frias, will benefit. It came at the perfect time for Raul. Russia's economy is in the tank. Venezuela no longer helps. It's like Obama is trying to rescue communism. There is a niece desperate to flee right now, but it's a bad time. Everyone is being watched. It's too risky right now."

I didn't care much for politics. I didn't watch television or listen to talk radio. I couldn't vote anymore. Back in the real world I had been conservative, both financially and socially. Surviving by growing and selling dope had changed my mind-set. I was a libertarian now, I supposed. I really didn't give a shit what you did. Live and let live. I did know enough to consider all Washington politicians to be either corrupt or idiotic. That much was clear. Bald Mark though, seemed to know what was going on.

"You are an interesting man, El Jefe," I said. "Not at all what I expected."

"I'm not a mafia goon," he said. "If that's what you expected. I'm educated. I stay up on the latest news, politics, and technology. I'm always one step ahead. I have to be. I call it awareness."

"I always thought I was pretty aware," I said. "But now I'm off the grid most of the time. Still, I know what's going on around me."

"I sensed that in you," he said. "You wouldn't have gotten to me, to even ask questions otherwise. You might be a little too alert, if that's possible."

"I have to stay one step ahead too," I said. "There are at least two law enforcement agencies that would love to get their hands on me."

He raised a non-existent eyebrow again.

"White collar crap," I said. "From a previous life."

"The Keys are full of guys like you," he said. "No big deal."

With that we were finished. I was in, even though I didn't want to be. I didn't know when he would call on me, or what he would have me do. I didn't want to do anything, except go and find Andi. For now, I had some time. I had some money. I'd leave right away.

Breeze on the High Seas

I spent the next day taking on fuel and water. I loaded *Leap of Faith* with food and beer. I even bought a bottle of rum for the trip. That night I studied charts and weather patterns. As the crow flies, it was seven hundred and fifty miles from Stock Island to Luperon. At seven knots, I'd be on the open seas for almost six days. I had never attempted such a voyage. I much preferred to hop from island to island. It felt safer to have the anchor down before dark and rest for the next day's run. I couldn't afford to do that this time. It had taken me months to island hop the Bahamas the last time I went to Luperon. I had no choice but to make a bee-line for the Dominican. I could doze with the autopilot engaged along the way.

I drew a straight line from the outer marker off Stock Island to the entrance to Luperon Harbor on my paper chart. I found it ironic that I'd be just off the Cuban coast for much of the trip. Twelve miles out was international waters, so I would be okay. There was no reason to make landfall in that country. Despite what Obama was trying to do, Americans were still forbidden to travel to Cuba. I played with the chart plotter for a while, entering waypoints to create a course. The boat was in fine shape and ready to cruise. I was confident she would get me there.

The weather was a different story. The next few days were perfect, but there was a disturbance in the Caribbean that got my attention. It hadn't formed into a tropical system yet, but it would need monitoring. Forecasts aren't much good out beyond three days, so I really didn't know what to expect. Cuba is only ninety miles south of Key West, but it's a long island. I wouldn't be free of its coastline for those three good days. If foul weather came up from the south, the island itself would afford some lee from the wind. I was going.

The Stock Island channel is broad, deep, and easily navigated. Its southernmost marker is flashing day beacon number two. I passed it on my port side and entered Hawk Channel. I couldn't steam due south towards Cuba, and I didn't need to anyway. Instead I ran southeast until I came to a spot where I could cross the reef. I pointed her bow straight for Luperon and engaged the autopilot. I watched intently for thirty minutes or so, making small adjustments in heading until I was certain we were on a perfect course. Then I laid back in the captain's chair and put my feet up on the helm. *Here we go Miss Leap. Take me to my money.*

After three days of nothing, except the open ocean, I was getting worn out. I had caught a few naps here and there, but I was really in need of a good sleep. I could make out the higher elevations of Cuba from time to time, but I had to stay offshore. I checked and rechecked our course and estimated time of arrival. I checked our distance from Cuban waters. Satisfied that all was well, I laid down to get some much needed rest. I slept like a dead man for four hours. I probably would have slept longer, but a change in the wind stirred me.

I climbed back to the bridge to take a look. The seas were kicking up a bit, but nothing we couldn't handle. The barometer had fallen some. There's a storm coming, I thought to myself. I could just barely see some dark clouds to the south and east of the island of Cuba. I kept my eyes on those clouds. They grew darker by the minute. The system seemed to be moving to the north.

I switch the VHF to scan, to see if I could pick up any chatter about the storm. Most of what I heard was in rapid Spanish that I couldn't understand. There were scattered English conversations in the background. I kept my eyes on the sky, and my ear to the radio. Amongst the crackles and static of the airwaves, I heard the words hurricane, and tornados. Well, blow me down, I thought. *You're awesome Breeze. You've been steering your vessel towards a hurricane.*

The wind was increasing in intensity. I kept studying the storm. I had almost reached the eastern edge of Cuba. I had no paper charts for Cuba. I scrolled the chartplotter ahead to get a look at what lie in front of me. The straits between Cuba and Haiti were very deep, which could mean big waves in a hurricane. I needed a place to hide, and quick.

Over the radio came an emergency announcement, in both Spanish and English. It was a caution to all mariners. Seek refuge immediately. A category three hurricane was traveling due north at ten knots towards the island of Hispaniola. Haiti was forecast to suffer a direct hit. The outer bands of the storm would reach from eastern Cuba to the Dominican Republican within a few hours. *Shit, shit, shit.*

I kept scrolling the chartplotter looking for a safe haven. I knew nothing about this island. I'd only ever heard of Havana and Guantanamo. If the storm was traveling north, I would be on its western edge. That meant I'd be getting winds from the north. I needed to get around the eastern point and go back west. That would put me further away from the center and give me shelter from north winds. That is, if I made it around before the storm hit. If I got caught out there in hurricane forces winds, I would be royally screwed.

I found what I was looking for, but it was a long way. Golfo De Guacanayobo looked like it was well protected. I shoved the throttle forward to increase speed. A few more knots of speed might make the difference. I veered off my original course and aimed for Punta Maisi, the northern tip of the east end of Cuba. The water was deep even close to shore. I could cut right around the point until I reached Nelson Bank, near Punta Negra. After that, I'd be in the lee of the island. It would take a few more hours to reach safe haven.

As I rounded the point, the wind really started whistling from the east. That meant the outer edge of the storm was upon me. The wind seemed to rush down from the mountains of Haiti and collide with the sea. I was getting hit on the port side with forty knot winds and waves over ten feet. *Leap of Faith* was not built for seas like this. She was a bit top-heavy and rolled precariously when broadsided by big waves. I had to zigzag several times to keep from capsizing in the larger wave sets. The wind was whipping the tops off the waves, sending salt spray at us hard.

The worst was yet to come, but I would soon be turning west and running away from the eye. After I skirted Nelson Bank, I could see an ominous looking military installation. I checked the chart to see what it was. It was Guantanamo Bay! The waves were now on my stern. Sailors wish each other following seas, but they wouldn't want these waves on their stern. Each one lifted us from back to front. One minute I was looking down, the next minute I was looking up. Walls of water rolled under our keel. Our speed on the way down each wave rose to ten knots. Going up would slow us down to four knots. I'm as salty as they come. I've never been sea sick, but this time I was starting to feel a little queasy.

I finally made it to the jutting point that forms Golfo De Guacanayobo. I turned hard to starboard and entered the bay. Cuba was not as mountainous as Hispaniola, but it was high enough to afford decent protection. The waves inside the bay decreased to five feet or less. Over the radio I heard another storm warning. It was still churning north, but had taken a slight jog to the west. The eye should pass directly between Cuba and Haiti. Not good. That was closer to me.

My next glance at the chartplotter puzzled me. There were no depths listed inside this bay. I was in sixty foot of water though, so I motored on. I wanted to get in close to something that would block the winds when it got real bad. Cayo Perla looked good. It was a small island off the town of Manzanillo. I steered for it. Suddenly the depths shrunk to ten feet. I slowed. The water was too churned up to see the bottom. At least now it was shallow enough to anchor. I crawled along at two knots with one eye on the depth finder. I got in pretty close to the little island in eight feet of water. Good enough.

I shifted to neutral and climbed down to prepare the anchor. I had a twenty kilogram Bruce on the bow, which meant forty-four pounds. I also had a forty-five pound CQR at the ready, with fifty foot of chain and two-hundred feet of rope attached. Once we lost forward momentum, I started lowering the Bruce. The wind caused us to drift back. I then lowered the CQR, and fed out line as we continue falling back. I put out almost all the rode I had. We came to an abrupt halt as the anchors dug in. I bridled off the main anchor, and secured the secondary anchor to the Sampson post. I returned to the bridge and shifted into reverse. Slowly at first, I backed down. Then I ran it up to almost full throttle to jam the anchors in the sand as firmly as I could. We didn't budge. I throttled down and shifted back to neutral. I went back to the bow and put some old fire hose around the rope rode, so it wouldn't chafe. I put more hose around the bridle lines.

The wind was howling now, but it seemed to be overhead. This was a great spot to ride it out, except for one thing. I was in Cuba. I did a rethink on my decision. What else could I have done? I would have never made it across to Haiti. It's a worse hell-hole than Cuba anyway. I could have tried turning north to Great Iguana, but the Bahamian authorities had me on a watch list. No, I did what I had to do. As soon as the storm passed, I'd haul ass out of here.

I battened the hatches and prepared for the worst. When I stopped moving, I realized how tired I was. I was hungry, but it was too rough to cook. The storm was really kicking now. Gusts were over a hundred knots. The old boat creaked and groaned, but the anchors were holding. If I did drag, it would be away from the island and further out into the bay. I fell asleep on the settee listening to the wind roar and the waves crash. When I awoke, the storm was over.

Caught in Cuba

I started the coffee pot to combat my grogginess. I took a quick inventory of the boat. Normally, *Leap of Faith* does not have any leaks. Apparently, she leaks during hurricanes. I mopped up as best I could and took a cup of coffee out onto the aft deck to watch the sunrise. It was nice here. Between cups I pumped the bilge dry and made ready to depart. It was still on the breezy side, but I couldn't hang around here.

I had just poured my second cup when I saw them coming. Six soldiers carrying rifles were crammed into a small boat. I guessed it wasn't a welcoming party. They pulled alongside and screamed at me in Spanish. I tried a few "no comprendos". Then I made out the word for "papers". I handed them my documents, such as they were. I hadn't renewed the Coast Guard documentation or the Florida registration. They asked for my passport, which was valid. I doubted the U.S. government had any contact with Cuba over white collar fugitives.

I should have been afraid, I suppose, but I was too exhausted to care. Besides, dealing with Bald Mark had been a more frightening experience than this. Eventually, they decided to arrest me. *Good job Breeze. You're going to a Cuban jail.*

They didn't take me to jail. I could make out every third or fourth word of their Cuban Spanish. I determined that they had been assigned to an undesirable, backwater station in the town of Sierra Maestra. They were on crap duty for whatever reason. They pretended to work while the Cuban government pretended to pay them. I had broken the monotony of their desolate lives. They had no cell to lock me up in, so I sat in a wooden chair in an office. They had sent for an interpreter.

While I waited, I recalled some poor guy who had rotted away in a Cuban jail for six years. He had recently been released thanks to Obama's overtures to

Raul Castro. They wouldn't turn over the convicted killers they were harboring, change their attitude towards civil rights, or hold democratic elections, but this one fellow was freed. Meanwhile, every day dozens of Cubans boarded leaky rafts and makeshift boats to escape the tyranny of the Castro regime. How bad must it be?

A new face entered the office. His uniform was crisply pressed and new. My captors' uniforms were wrinkled and threadbare. He was obviously more important than they were. He didn't offer to shake hands or exchange pleasantries with me.

"I am Colonel Hernandez," he said, in perfect English. "It is not a good time to create an incident in our country. What are you doing here?"

"I'm not trying to cause an incident," I said. "I was just seeking shelter from the storm. I had no place to go. I didn't intend to set foot in your country. Your men forced me to set foot in Cuba."

"In Cuba, we consider our territorial waters as part of our country," he replied. "We take trespass very seriously, as you must know."

Ed Robinson

"I understand completely, sir," I said. "I had no intention of coming here, but the storm drove me in. I would have lost my boat, probably died. I had no choice."

"I believe you call it, any harbor in a storm, no?" he asked.

"Except for Cuba, I guess," I answered.

He had been standing with his arms crossed. Now he put on hand under his chin, considering what to do about me, I guessed.

"I would be inclined to return you to your vessel and escort you to international waters," he said. "But I have no such authority."

My heart sunk. I hung my head and let out a long sigh.

"I'm sorry, but I must notify Havana," he said.

Now I was afraid. He started barking orders to the other men, in Spanish. My mind was racing. *How are you going to get out of this one, Breeze?*

"General Frias," I said, quite loudly. "Let me speak to Leopoldo Frias."

The room went silent and all eyes turned to me. Just the sound of his name put fear into these men. Even the colonel seemed shaken.

"How do you know of general Frias?" he asked.

"Mutual friends," I answered. "He may wish to speak with me, I don't know."

He put his hand under his chin again. I let him think.

"Actually, that may be a better option than Raul," he said. "The general is an intelligent man, a reasonable man. He will understand the need to keep this quiet."

"Thank you," I said.

"Do not thank me," he replied. "It will be up to the general to decide. He may not wish to speak to you. You may end up in prison, or worse. You could not have picked a worse time to stumble into Cuba."

I hoped that the current political situation would discourage the Cuban government from mistreating me.

Why take me prisoner when they are working on normalizing relations with America? There was no need to create an international incident over a lowly boat bum like me. I wasn't worth the hassle, the way I saw it. The general kept me waiting for twenty-four hours.

When he entered the office, I was surprised at how old he was. Then I remembered that Fidel, if he was still alive, was well into his nineties. Raul was getting up there in age as well. Bald Mark had told me that Frias was pals with Raul, so they were probably about the same age.

"Senor Breeze," he said. "Please, tell me about our mutual friend. Why have you asked for me? I don't need this right now. You put me in an awkward position."

"I work for bald Mark," I said.

"That would explain why the dogs thought you had drugs onboard your vessel," he said. "We searched it quite thoroughly, but found nothing. You carried drugs for senor Mark recently, no?"

"I did," I admitted. "But that was in Florida. I am here on my own time."

"I will have to contact him in Florida," he said. "We share a mutual respect, regardless of how he makes his living."

He turned and walked out. No goodbyes, no instructions, no nothing. I had bought some time. He didn't toss me in jail, yet. How would Bald Mark react to the news that I was in Cuba? Would he throw me to the wolves, or would he vouch for me? How did I continue to find myself in these perilous positions?

Colonel Hernandez returned with good news. Frias had told him to handle me with care until he decided what to do. A guard had been posted at my boat. It would make a nice target for those wishing to escape the island. I was given a good meal of roast chicken with rice and beans. The café con leche was excellent, as was the fresh Cuban bread. A cot was set up in the back room, and I slept like Rip Van Winkle. I had high hopes that Frias would set me free. I wasn't so sure about Bald Mark.

The next day, Frias returned. I hadn't expected that. I had figured he would just relay the word through Hernandez. I soon found out why he had decided to deliver his message personally. My release was conditional. Bald Mark had indeed vouched for me, but was quite curious about my little adventure. Ever the businessman, he had negotiated a deal with Frias. I was to smuggle the niece out of the country, and deliver her to Bald Mark. That smart bastard had figured out a way to gain my freedom, make some money in the deal, and further endear himself to the general. I had to give him credit. It was brilliant.

"My niece, senor Breeze," said the general. "Yolanda Aldama. She is as pure as the virgin mother. You will see to her safety and continued purity in exchange for your release."

"I will get her to Florida in one piece," I said. "Don't worry, and thank you."

"Your thanks should go to senor Mark," he said. "But your misadventure has proved to be a blessing. Vaya con Dios, Yolanda."

Her gave her a hug and kissed her on the forehead. She whispered in his ear, and then she touched his cheek as he departed. She turned to me and shrugged her shoulders.

"Now what?" she asked.

"You are to leave immediately," said Colonel Hernandez. "My men have filled your boat with diesel and fresh water. Go now. May God be with you both."

Yolanda didn't speak during the ride to the harbor. I kept sneaking glances at her. She was pretty, no doubt about it. She was probably half my age, maybe late twenties. Her cinnamon skin was flawless. She had big, round, brown eyes above rounded cheek bones. Her hair was a very light shade of brown, not quite blond. It fell around her face and below her shoulders, sometimes hiding her eyes. Her figure was curvy. There was no excess weight, but she was rounded in all the right places, ripe. She reminded me of some Mexican girls I once knew. Their hot young bodies become plump old bodies later in life.

She wore a simple peasant dress, with a wide belt cinched around her waist. He shoes were plain, black flats. She carried one lone satchel that she slung over her shoulder as she walked. It looked heavy, but she didn't labor with it. She sat demurely with her hands in her lap. Her posture was erect, proud.

She still hadn't spoken when we boarded *Leap of Faith*. I took her bag and showed her the berth. She said a simple thank you and closed the door behind her. It felt strange to have a woman on board again, especially one who didn't speak.

As I pulled up the anchors, my thoughts turned to my now failed mission. I wasn't continuing on to Luperon. Instead, I was going back to Florida to face Bald Mark. He had saved my ass. I couldn't cross him now. Plus, there was the girl. I had to get her to America, or both Bald Mark and a Cuban General would be hunting me.

I tried to look at the bright side. I had survived a hurricane and avoided a Cuban jail. My new cargo was a pretty senorita. I wondered if I'd get a cut from this human trafficking escapade.

Another fine mess, Breeze.

Senorita Smuggling

When I rounded the cape at Punta Maisi, my escorts fell away. I was on my own, except for Yolanda. Eventually she came up on the bridge and sat down in the mate's chair.

"How long will it take?" she asked.

"She speaks!" was my reply.

"I am sorry," she said. "I don't know you. I don't know what my future holds. I've left my family behind, and I'm a little bit afraid."

"It took me almost three full days to get to Manzanillo," I said. "Relax. The weather looks good.

Enjoy the ride. Thank you for choosing *Leap of Faith* cruises."

"I didn't choose any of this," she said.

My attempt at lightening her mood didn't work. Instead she began to cry. When it looked as if her crying would continue for a while, I engaged the autopilot and went to her. I took her in my arms, but she stiffened. What else can you do when a woman is crying? She gently pushed me away and tried to choke back her tears.

"I didn't want this," she said. "I love Cuba. I love my family."

"Why then?" I asked.

"A very important man made advances towards me," she started. "I said no. He is a vile, old pervert. He disgusts me."

"What's the big deal?" I asked. "Happens all the time in America."

"Cuba is different," she said. "You don't say no to the politicos, or the generals. My uncle protects me from the military, but he has no sway with the politicos, other than Raul. Even Raul wouldn't care what happened to a peasant girl."

"So you are on the bad side of the Party, because you wouldn't sleep with some old asshole?"

"Please, do not swear," she said. "But yes, life becomes unbearable once the Party targets you."

I knew, that as a political refugee, once she stepped foot on American soil, she was welcome to apply for a visa. As long as I delivered her safely to land, she would have legal status. *New Mission, Breeze.* For once, I was performing a selfless act. I was actually going to do something good and worthy for a change.

"You'll be fine," I said. "I promise. I'll take care of you."

She looked me in the eyes. Her cheeks were still wet. She studied me, trying to decide if I was trustworthy or not. The longer I looked at her, the more beautiful she became. Her look was one that grows on you.

"Just get me to Florida," she said. "That's all I ask."

I went back to the helm and tried to busy my mind by checking all the gauges.

She had given no indication that she was attracted to me. She was kind of cold, actually. I guessed I was too old for her. Getting involved with her would be a huge mistake anyway. Not that I wasn't prone to poor choices. No, I had to keep it strictly business. I'd square up with Bald Mark, see what happens next. I remembered what the General had said about preserving her purity.

Over the next two days, her mood improved. She squealed with delight when a pod of dolphins danced in our bow wake. She brought me sandwiches and drinks when I needed them. She even cleaned house down in the salon. She had dusted, washed the windows, and swept the floor. She said she just wanted to keep busy. I appreciated her efforts. I wasn't much of a housekeeper, but the Cubans had made a mess when they ransacked the boat looking for drugs.

When she wanted to take a shower, I started to lecture her about not using too much water. She told me that in Cuba, they were lucky if the water ran at all. Electricity was the same. Sometimes it worked and sometimes it didn't. A hot shower was a luxury in her country, one that a peasant girl may never experience. That softened me up. We had just topped off the water tanks, and when the boat is underway the engine heats the water. I told her to take as long as she wanted. I didn't want her to smell like me. I hadn't had a shower since I left Florida. Maybe that's why she wasn't interested in me.

As she bathed, I pictured her naked body just a few feet away. I drew a mental picture of her lathering herself, focusing on the good parts. The clothes she wore didn't reveal much. I caught an occasional glimpse of an ankle. No cleavage, no leg above the calf. I knew she had to have a nice body under those frumpy dresses though. She carried herself with a quiet dignity. She spoke English better than I did, using proper grammar with few contractions. There was also the hint that she was a virgin. That would be hard to imagine in America. The only adult virgins in our country are those too ugly to attract a partner. It all gave her a mystique that drove me wild. I was hot for her. Although she was friendlier now, she still had given no sign that she felt the same about me.

When she came back to the bridge, she was wearing jeans and a western shirt. It was the kind with those pearl snaps like cowboys wear. She had snapped every last one right up to her neck. The jeans were tight, so they gave me a better look at her figure. It was very nice. She had a high, round ass that stayed firm when she moved. Her breasts were larger than average, but not huge. I didn't like huge boobs anyway. Everything was perfectly proportioned. She wasn't hard and flat. She was soft, without being chubby.

She was brushing her still wet hair when I finally spoke.

"Did you enjoy your shower?" I asked.

"Very much, thank you," she replied. "Best shower I ever had. I didn't want it to end."

My mind flashed back to the mental image of her wet and naked, but I suppressed it. As if she could read my mind, she said it felt weird showering so close to a man she didn't know. If she had been an American girl, I would have confessed to picturing her naked. I'd try to break the ice, get a reaction. But she was different. I bit my tongue.

Instead I changed the subject.

"What will happen when we get to Florida?" I asked.

"This man Mark is supposed to take me to Miami. There are Cubans there who will help me."

"So, do you have any family in the states?" I asked.

"No, not in Miami," she said. "I have distant relatives in Baltimore."

"Neither Baltimore or Miami are nice places," I told her. "But better than Cuba I suppose."

"I am told that Miami is a beautiful city," she said. "There are many Cubans living there. They have good jobs, nice homes, and happy lives."

"I suppose that is true," I said. "But there is a lot of crime and craziness in Miami."

"I suppose I will find out for myself, soon enough," she said.

She pointed to the northwest. I could just make out the city skyline. You can see Miami from a long way off from the water, especially at night. We weren't going to Miami though. It was my job to deliver Yolanda to Bald Mark. After that, I was out of the picture. I'd wish her well and be on my way.

What about Bald Mark? How would I handle him? I thought about that for a few minutes. Eventually I decided that I'd anchor somewhere in the Keys and call him. I'd see how the call went. I'd get my instructions, and go from there. I decided on Islamorada. I'd take Yolanda to the Lorelie and show her off. Maybe I'd buy her a new dress first, something more American.

The rest of the trip was uneventful. She asked me a lot of questions about American culture. I didn't have much nice to say, but I tempered it for her. She was getting excited. I could sense her nervousness too. Dropping a simple Cuban farm girl into Miami would be like dropping me on Mars. Everything would be foreign, especially our excesses.

As soon as I dropped the hook she came to me.

"I must go to shore immediately," she said urgently. "I must touch American soil."

"Okay, okay," I said. "Keep your pants on. We'll be on shore in a few minutes."

I lowered the dinghy and made it ready to go. I double checked the anchor rode, and peaked in the bilge. All was good. I felt rushed but I understood her need to get to land. She could barely contain herself as we rode in to the restaurant. There is a small sandy landing in the mangroves perfect for beaching a dinghy. Our bow rolled up on the sand and she leapt out. She stomped around in the sand in her bare feet with her hands in the air.

"I am in America!" she sang out. "I am in America."

I felt so happy for her that I picked her up in a bear hug and swung her around in circles. Instead of resisting, she hugged me back. She put her head on my shoulder and squeezed me tight. I could feel her breasts against my chest. I could smell her freshly washed hair. I stopped spinning but held the embrace.

"Thank you, Breeze," she said. "I can never repay you. Thank you so much."

Then she kissed me. It was just a quick peck, but it was on the lips. I felt a little guilty. I didn't volunteer to bring her to America. I did it to save my own sorry ass.

"Come on," I said. "Let's go have a drink."

I pulled a stool out for her at the bar. She gave me a slight curtsy before taking her seat. She had no idea what to order. She'd never had an alcoholic beverage in her life. She told me that a beer cost a week's pay in Havana. I asked if she even wanted booze. She said she didn't think she did, so I ordered her a Shirley Temple. I got a beer. She asked the barmaid her name. When the lady replied, she told her that she was from Cuba. She would like the barmaid to verify that she had indeed set foot on American soil, if it ever became necessary. It was a smart idea. We might get boarded later on the boat. Anything can happen in the Keys. A change had come over her. We sat and talked and ordered more drinks. She was relaxed. We walked down to the little beach and stood by the dinghy to watch the sunset. As that fiery ball sank into the waters of Florida Bay, she reached over and took my hand.

"It's beautiful, Breeze," she said.

At that moment in time, I wanted to grab her and kiss her forever. I wanted to hold her and protect her from all the dangers of the world. She was so innocent, and so naïve. Miami would chew her up and spit her out. She'd never be as pure as she was at that instant. I didn't act on my impulses.

"Come on," I said. "I want to get back to the boat before dark. I still have to call Bald Mark."

I had a bad feeling about a reunion with him.

Saving Yolanda

I made the call to Bald Mark. I didn't know if he'd be furious with me, or happy to have swung such a deal with the Cuban general. My predicament, and the fact that I dropped his name in an attempt to save myself, had handed him a golden opportunity. Maybe he'd be thankful.

"What in the hell were you doing in Cuba?" was the first thing out of his mouth.

I had practiced my lie before calling him.

"I was picking up some Bahamian shit off Great Iguana," I said. "Or at least I was supposed to. Storm drove me to shelter."

He knew I had been running pot. He didn't know where I got it from.

"That was quick thinking asking to talk to Frias," he said. "I was surprised to hear from him. Even more surprised to learn that you were in the custody of the Cuban military."

"I guess I owe you my thanks," I said.

"Well, yes," he said. "I did get you out of a jam. You could have spent years sitting in jail down there. On the other hand, I made out like a bandit."

"I have to hand it to you," I said. "Sending the girl back with me, that whole deal to get me out of the country, was a stroke of genius on your part."

"I told you I was no dumbass," he said. "Where are you? I need to take the girl off your hands."

He didn't sound like he was out to murder me. He had even chuckled during the conversation. Could I trust him? I really had no choice. I told him where we were. He said he'd send Enrique to pick her up.

"Does it have to be that sleaze-ball?" I asked. "He gives me the creeps. I know the girl won't like him."

"The rest of them are worse," he said. "This ain't no daycare center. Just sit tight. Wait for him."

I told Yolanda to ready her things, and we waited. She sat like she'd done back in Cuba. Her hands were in her lap, and her head was down. I could hear the go-fast boat long before I could see it. I dreaded handing her over, but she really wasn't my problem.

As he slowed the boat to approach us, Yolanda grabbed me by the arm and looked at me. Her eyes showed gratitude, but also fear.

"I will never see you again?" she asked.

"Very doubtful," I said. "I never go to Miami."

"Thank you Breeze," she said. "I don't know how you came to associate with bad men, because you are not bad."

"It's been a pleasure meeting you, Yolanda," I said.

I gave her a quick hug, releasing her to grab a line from Rick. He banged his boat into mine a little hard for my liking. I made him wait while I threw out some fenders.

"Hurry up, man," he yelled. "We got work to do."

"Work?" I asked. "You were just supposed to pick up the girl."

"We have another pickup to make," he said.

"Coke?" I asked. "With her on board?"

"More Cubans," he answered. "The guys are bringing them in on the fast boats. We pick them up, take them all to Tavernier. I guess your little Cuban adventure spurred the general to let more people go."

It took a minute for that to sink in. I'd gone from selling home-grown dope and a little homemade rum, to smuggling cocaine, to human trafficking. How else could I break the law? It didn't seem that bad taking one pretty girl on a boat ride from Cuba to Florida. Delivering a boatload of refugees somehow seemed more illegal. I felt bad for the Cuban people though. The general had let me go. Bald Mark had helped me to escape. I supposed a few more Cubans in Miami wouldn't make much of a difference.

I fired up the diesel and started pulling up the anchor. Rick had told me to head for Rodriguez Key, which wasn't far. It was just south of Key Largo on the ocean side. We'd be in back in Bald Mark's marina in no time.

"Have you had a piece of that fine ass yet?" asked Rick. "Because I'm gonna tap it. Just wanted to know if I was getting your sloppy seconds."

"Leave her alone," I said. "I don't think El Jefe would be happy if he knew you had raped the general's niece."

He laughed at me like I'd told a hysterical joke.

"You are so stupid, newbie," he said. "All of us will have a turn, the bald man too. Then we dump them all in Little Havana. Small price to pay for their freedom from the Castros."

This was a horrible turn of events. I couldn't let it happen. I'd grown quite fond of her. I had to figure out a way to protect her. I thought she'd have a hard time in Miami, but now she was about to be raped aboard my own boat. She hadn't even been in America for twenty-four hours yet.

Enrique left the bridge and climbed down the ladder. I couldn't help noticing just how much bigger he was than me. He was a nasty character, that I had no hopes of beating in hand-to-hand combat. I'd had exactly one physical confrontation in twenty years. Andi and I had managed to knock two purse snatchers in the water. This was a different challenge. I needed some kind of weapon. I looked around the bridge for something to hit him with. I heard Yolanda scream. *Jesus, Breeze. You have got to be the most fucked up person on the planet. Do something!*

Then I remembered my tool bag. It was in the console under the helm. I didn't have any wrenches big enough to do the trick. What else was in there? I grabbed a hammer. When I first put my tools aboard, I'd wondered what I'd ever need a hammer for. Glad I held on to it. I could hear scuffling coming from the salon. I stuck my head down through the hatch and saw Yolanda's naked breasts. He had ripped her shirt open and was trying to pull her jeans down. There was a red hand imprint on her cheek. She was crying and saying No, no, no.

I pulled my head back up and shouted down below.

"Hey Rick," I said. "You better come up here. We got trouble."

"I'm busy, asshole," he said.

"I'm serious," I said. "The Coast Guard, three boats. Just sitting there waiting."

I heard someone run forward and slam the door to the stateroom. He must have let her go. I waited by the hatch. I heard the big Latino coming and readied my hammer. He was coming up the ladder. As soon as I saw the top of his head, I smashed it in. I heard his skull crack, felt the sponginess inside. He plopped onto the deck like a sack of rocks.

I looked at the hammer. There was no blood or gray matter on it. I dropped it overboard anyway. The feeling of cracking a skull was making me nauseous. I shook it off and ran to Yolanda.

"It's okay," I said. "I knocked him out. Maybe killed him."

She flung open the door and jumped into my arms. She hugged me hard and cried uncontrollably. I had to push her away. There was a dead body, or at least a severely injured bad guy sprawled on the deck. We both went to investigate. He wasn't dead. He hadn't moved, but he was breathing.

Now I was in a whole new pickle. What do I do with him? If I threw him overboard, he would die. I couldn't call for a rescue for any number of reasons. I was the one who brained him for starters. I was on the run from the law, for seconds. I was harboring a Cuban refugee that would cause a lot of questions, Lorelie barmaid or not.

"Just throw him overboard," said Yolanda. "Feed him to the sharks."

"I can't do it," I said. "I've never killed a man. Don't really want to add murder to my list of sins."

I went to the bow and started unbuckling the straps that held the life raft. I had no idea if it would actually inflate. It was years past its inspection date, but when I pulled the cord, it starting inflating right away. I tied it off behind the swim platform. Lugging the lifeless body was a chore. I half rolled him, half lifted him through the transom door. I pulled the raft up close and used my feet to shove him onto it. I heard a soft moan from the raft when he landed. I tossed a couple bottles of water in after him, then hesitated. Would he make it? Did I care? Then I threw my hand-held VHF in with him. If he came to, he could call for help. If he never woke up, well, fuck him. I untied the raft and kicked it free. I finally felt safe. The entire time I was moving him, I kept thinking he would wake up and kick my ass, busted skull and all.

Now what? I had just clobbered Bald Mark's number one man. Sure, I did it to stop a rape, but apparently that rape was sanctioned by the boss. I couldn't take Yolanda to him. Even if I managed to talk my way out of this mess, he'd abuse the girl himself. I turned to Yolanda.

"I can take you to Miami," I said. "But we have to be fast. Sooner or later Mark's other men will get tired of waiting for us."

"What about the other Cubans?" she asked.

"They know Rick is supposed to be with me," I said. "We can't help them. They will have to take them to shore in the fast boats."

"There is nothing in Miami for me," she said. "Rick told me that it was all a lie. They would dump me in Little Havana when they were finished with me."

"I don't know what to do," I said.

"My debt to you continues to grow, Breeze," she said. "I knew you were a good man. I cannot repay you, but please, please help me."

"I'll think of something," I muttered, as she came into my arms.

We held each other for a long time, gently swaying with the motion of the boat. Her heart beat slowed as she rested in my arms. My life had been full of dramatic turns, now here was another one. I was in charge of another human life. I was responsible for her. I had only wanted to get her to America and be done with it. That was impossible now, it seemed. On the bright side, she had touched my heart, gotten under my skin. She was so nice to look at. She had a sweet and gentle soul. She hadn't been corrupted by modern society like American women. She made me long for simpler times. I should take her away to some tropical island to live together in peace, if she would have me. Then I remembered Andi. Then I remembered my money. I gently drew Yolanda away from me and held her at arm's length.

"What do you think about Luperon?" I asked.

Another Shot at Luperon

I explained the whole story to Yolanda as I set a course for Tavernier Creek. The marinas in Key Largo were closer, but I'd have to pass Rodriguez Key, and Bald Mark's men, to get to them. I needed fuel and water. I also needed good weather information. I didn't want to run into another storm anywhere near Cuba. Taking Yolanda near Cuban waters was a risk in itself. We had to move fast, but I needed to think.

We tied up at the fuel dock at Tavernier Creek Marina. We were dangerously close to Blue Waters, and Bald Mark. It put me on edge, a feeling I was accustomed to. I took my charts to the dayroom along with my laptop. The simplest thing to do, would be to island hop the Bahamas. I couldn't check in with Customs though. I studied the charts and Googled up a list of Immigration offices in the Bahamas. We'd have to skip the major developed islands to avoid Customs. It would make for long passages with no opportunity to provision. We needed lots of food.

I went back to the boat and dug out the coffee can. I instructed Yolanda to take one of the dock carts, and go buy was much food as she could handle. I peeled off five hundred dollars bills. She just stared at the money.

"Are you a rich man, Breeze?" she asked.

"Do you understand the American dollar?" I asked back.

"Yes," she said. "But it's so much money."

"You'll be fine," I told her. "Buy whatever you want."

She kissed me on the cheek, tucked the bills in her bra, and walked off with the cart. The peck on the cheek and seeing her fingers in her cleavage gave me a flushed feeling. I had seen her breasts in worse times, and they were very nice. Breeze junior began to stir. *Stop it, Breeze. You're twice her age.* I went back to my charts.

We could make a very long run to Andros in good weather. We'd have to bypass Georgetown, which was a shame. I would have loved to visit with my old friend Captain Fred. We could anchor in Salt Pond, Calabash Bay, and Conception. We'd skip Rum Cay and Mayaguana, instead making a really long jump south to Great Iguana. From there it was a doable hundred miles or so to Luperon. We'd never be near Cuban waters.

The weather was perfect. The forecast called for light south winds and then no wind at all over the next three days. I topped off the water tanks after the fuel tanks were filled. The boat could use some attention, but I didn't have time. I couldn't linger here. I'd run her hard to Cuba and back. She needed an oil change and new fuel filters. I went up to the ship's store to get what I needed. When I came back, Yolanda was pushing an overflowing dock cart towards the boat. What is it with women? Fruits and vegetables spilled out of their bags. I saw tortillas, flour and sugar. Finally as we stored the groceries, I saw chicken and beef. I could catch some fish along the way.

"I have never seen so much food," she said. "America is a wonderland. I still have three hundred dollars."

"You keep it," I said. "Just to have."

"Oh, I cannot," she said. "I owe you so much already."

"Suit yourself," I said. I put the bills back in the coffee can and prepared to shove off.

I looked at the clock. We were supposed to be meeting the fast boats right about then. How long would they wait? They only way to get by them, without being seen, was to run due south and cut through the reef, before turning east. My chart showed deep water just to the east of Conch Reef. I made a beeline for it. If Mark's men waited for two hours, I'd be fourteen miles out to sea, well beyond the reef. It's a big, big ocean out there. They'd be stuck with Cuban passengers, and desperate to offload them someplace. I thought of the possible scenarios. What if they put all the passengers on one boat, and sent the others to look for us? I didn't think it was likely, but it was possible. These guys weren't real bright, but Bald Mark was.

What would he do when I didn't show up with the girl? What would he do when Rick never returned, or washed up on a beach somewhere? I was toast with Bald Mark. Terry had told me not to cross him. It's not like I wasn't warned. Again it amazed me, how a simple boat bum could lead such a complicated life. I was beginning to feel cursed. I had made some bad decisions sure, but the storm hadn't been my fault. Having the girl thrust on me wasn't my choice. The attempted rape wasn't my idea either. Now, I wasn't only running from the law, I was also running from a criminal mastermind who ruled over the entire Florida Keys. *Brilliant Breeze.*

My pity party was interrupted by the pop of a beverage can opening. Yolanda brought me a cold beer and a sandwich. We were two hours out, well beyond the reef and heading east. It was almost dark. I'd feel safer out here in the dark of the night. I'd run with no lights. If anyone was searching for us, we'd be tough to find. No one would expect us to head due south, in the direction of Cuba.

I set up two deck chairs on the bridge facing aft, so we could watch the sunset. There was not another boat in sight. The seas were flat. Our wake stretched out behind us to infinity. Who knew what the future might bring, but at that moment, I breathed it all in. I was the captain of a good boat. I was in the company of a fine woman. The sun was sizzling into a glass, calm sea. This life I had chosen had these moments. They sustained me.

"What will you do after Luperon?" asked Yolanda.

"I don't know," I answered. "But hopefully, I'll have plenty of money to do it."

"I hope it works out for you, Breeze," she said. "Whatever you decide to do."

"My question is, what will we do with you?" I said.

"I don't know either," she replied. "I have no place to go. If I return to Cuba, they will put me in prison, and probably arrest my uncle. He is taking too many chances to free his loved ones. I will have to make a life for myself, somewhere."

"We have plenty of time to decide, each of us," I said. "We are taking the long way around to get to Luperon. It will be a beautiful trip. You'll need to learn to relax. Let your hair down a little."

I told her what I knew of the Bahamas. I described the serene beaches and the sparkling waters I had seen with Andi. I talked of quiet nights, alone in deserted anchorages, lying back and looking at the stars. I tried to sell her on the idea of living on a boat.

"I don't even have a bathing suit," she said, out of the blue.

"You don't need one in the Bahamas," I chuckled. "Just disrobe and jump in."

"I could never do that," she said. "I have never even worn a bikini."

"We'll have to work on that," I said. "Can't get much of a tan in those dresses you wear."

"I'm already darker than you," she laughed. "I don't need a suntan."

She was right about that, and I was pretty tan for a Caucasian. Cubans came in all varieties. Some were black as coal, their blood lines having mixed with African, Jamaican, or some other Caribbean tribe. She had some Indian blood in her I guessed, maybe Mayan or something equally exotic. I couldn't wait to see her in a bikini. When it came to pretty women, I was an equal opportunity lecher. Pretty was pretty, as far as I was concerned, no matter the nationality.

I had lost track of all the girls I'd slept with over the years, but that all ended when I'd met Laura. She won me over, well and good. I devoted my life to her and to her only. I'd never strayed. She caused me to find a place in my heart that I'd never known existed. Her love cured me of the restlessness and unease that had forever plagued me. Now she was gone. She was gone and I was traipsing about the seven seas, talking to her ashes.

I went and got the film canister that contained what was left of her. I told Yolanda more of my sad tale. I didn't leave anything out. She just sat and listened, didn't ask any questions. When I was finished, she spoke.

"You are unlike any man I've ever known," she said. "You are a mystery. You are obviously an intelligent, honest, and caring man. But you deal in a dark world of drugs and crime. You must find a way out, Breeze. Inside, I know you are good."

"The only good thing I've done lately is save you," I said. "First from Cuba, and now from that monster Enrique. Neither was a choice I made. It was just something I had to do."

"You could have let him take me," she said. "He would kill you in a fight. There would be no shame in that."

"Oh yes there would," I said. "I've faced enough shame. I would have died first."

"And that is why you are a good man, Breeze," she said.

With that, we went silent.

The Bahamas

We approached Andros Island near Miller Creek on the southwest side. The west coast of Andros is not like the rest of the Bahamas. It is heavily forested in pines and other hardwoods like mahogany and lignum vitae. Mangroves crowd the shore, denying access over most of the coastline. My chart showed dozens of tricky shoals, so we slowed to a crawl as we got nearer. I stationed Yolanda on the bow to watch for rocks and coral. She was wearing shorts that she had made by cutting off a pair of jeans. I would have liked them to be shorter, but she cut them a few inches above the knee. She was wearing one of her cowgirl shirts, tied up above the waist to reveal her belly. She had the sleeves rolled up. It wasn't exactly nautical attire, but it was an improvement over those shapeless dresses.

We were one hundred and seventy miles from Miami and we were both tired. I had chosen this stop for its remoteness. No one lives here, or even comes for a visit. It is a desolate and foreboding place. I didn't plan to hang around, but it was reassuring to know that no one would ever find us here. We could relax. After securing the anchor, I grabbed a beer and lounged on the aft deck. Yolanda joined me. She was staring at the tangled snarl of vegetation on shore.

"It's not exactly paradise," she said. "It's kind of eerie."

"We'll move over to Sampson Cay tomorrow," I told her. "It's pretty. Nice beach. You'll like it much better."

Just then a terrible screeching noise cracked the silence. It was coming from the island. Yolanda jumped in fright. It startled me a bit too, but I knew what it was. That's what I told her anyway.

"It's a chickcharnie," I declared.

"A what?" she asked.

"A chickcharnie is a red-eyed Bahamian elf with three toes, feathers, and a beard. They are mischievous little devils. They live in the trees here."

"You are making that up," she said.

"I am not," I said. "It's why the place is uninhabited. The ancient Arawaks tried to live here, but they were all killed or run off by the chickcharnies. The Spanish tried too. There isn't even a sign of their settlement."

"Such a creative mind," she said. "Wasted on a boat bum."

"I didn't create the chickcharnies," I insisted. "They've long been a part of Bahamian folklore. Parents still threaten their kids with them. Like the boogieman or something."

"I'm glad we are leaving this place tomorrow," she said. "It's so rugged and mysterious looking."

"We need to get some rest," I said. "Sampson Cay is a very long way off. As soon as the sun goes down, I'm going to bed."

We sat in silence as the setting sun painted the sky with orange, red, and purple. It is a rare chance to witness a sunset with no land to block your view. At these latitudes, the sun is huge as it slowly sinks into the ocean. The Green Flash is a common occurrence here, and we experienced the most brilliant example anyone has ever seen. It was as if the sun shone up through the water, blasting laser beams of green from beneath the surface. It snapped back at us like emerald lightning bolts. I stood and started applauding. Yolanda stood and took my arm. It was magnificent.

Just to the northwest of Staniel Cay and just to the southeast of the Exuma National Land and Sea Park lies tiny Sampson Cay. The waters surrounding it have been called the most beautiful cruising waters in the world. It is what you dream of, the stuff postcards and calendars are made of. It is also remote enough not to have a Customs office. The only thing there is the Sampson Cay Club. It's a resort and marina with a small community-like atmosphere. Here we topped off on fuel and water. I wanted to buy Yolanda a bikini, but we searched the ship's store and grocery store in vain.

The next day we took the dinghy along the shore until we found an empty stretch of beach. I managed to coax Yolanda into the water, wearing her bra and panties. She covered herself with a towel until she was right at the water's edge. I got a three-second glimpse of her before she was neck deep in the water. She made my loins ache. We played the day away, splashing and floating to our hearts content. We were a million miles from bad men or IRS agents. I was amused by Yolanda's modesty, but I respected her wishes. Andi had been completely carefree about nudity, even in public. I was somewhere in the middle on the issue. I'll show you mine if you show me yours.

The following days played out much the same. We worked our way south through the Exumas, avoiding major ports of call, and crowded anchorages. We stayed to ourselves, sunning on the white beaches and playing in the water. I caught fresh fish, which Yolanda expertly prepared. We continued sharing sunsets, but went our separate ways at bedtime. We did not share intimate conversations about the meaning of life, or what our futures might hold. We were removed from the world, shedding the stress and the worries that come with it. I could stay this way forever, but I'd need the money to make that happen.

At the end of the first week, we had reached the end of the Exumas. The entrance to Georgetown harbor taunted me as we passed it by. It would have been great to see old friends, take safe haven and enjoy the circus that is Georgetown. It was too risky, though. Customs is aware of every vessel. Folks know your business. I couldn't take the chance of being found out. We motored on for Salt Pond, on Long Island.

Cruising from Georgetown, I continued easterly along the north shore of Hog Cay, leaving the north shore of White Cay a mile to starboard. Once abeam of White Cay's east end, I turned to one hundred, fourteen on the compass dial. This carried us clear of the White Cay Bank, and we saw seven foot of water all the way to Indian Hole Point. This anchorage offered us the best protection on the west coast of Long Island, and made a good jumping off point for destinations further south. I had changed my mind about visiting Rum and Conception. They were on the recommended cruising route, but I wanted a more direct path south. Instead, I decided on running straight for the Crooked Islands. From there we could stage at Acklins Island for a run to Great Iguana.

Once settled in Salt Pond, we walked up the street to Harding's Supply Center. It was an eclectic shop full of groceries, house wares, drugs, marine and fishing supplies and even lumber. We found a rack of bathing suits and Yolanda took a few items to the changing room to try on. I waited patiently, hoping she would model them for me, but she did not. She chose a black two-piece job, that I couldn't really call a bikini. It featured a modest bottom that covered everything, with a top that had fringe hanging down almost to her waist. It was tight though, and really highlighted her curves. It would do.

I got to see a lot of it in the Ragged Islands. This island group, a mini-archipelago, comprises the southeastern limit of the Great Bahama Bank. It runs in a half-moon shape for one hundred miles. Little Ragged Island is the southernmost scrap of land at the bottom of the crescent. It's the backwaters of the Bahamas. Dozens of unimportant, uninhabited cays are strung about the crystal waters. It was the perfect place for two fugitives to hide. We explored for a week, never seeing another vessel except the mail boat that runs to Potter's Cay.

Yolanda shed some of her shyness there. We were getting more comfortable with each other. She was getting more comfortable in her skin. She wore the bathing suit constantly. Her brown skin was even darker now. Her newfound playfulness allowed me to enjoy her company without constantly thinking about her body. Some couples, after being stuck on a boat for weeks, can come to hate each other. We became friends. We were all each other had. We were alone together in a tropical paradise, sharing our sexless friendship. *Great Breeze, you have a sister now.*

We saw No Bush Cay, Dead Cay, Sisters Cay, Nurse Cay, Double-Breasted Cay (my favorite), and Hog Cay. There was a Raccoon Cay, as well as Raccoon

Cut, and a lighthouse on Flamingo Cay. Eventually I grew anxious to make progress towards the Dominican Republic. We set off for Great Iguana, which was almost uninhabited. The only place we'd have trouble, would be in Luperon itself.

Great Iguana is a large island, which is flatter than most of the others in the Bahamas. We could see the stacks at the Morton Salt Factory from the bridge. It's in another world. We felt like we were in some sort of Jurassic Park for flamingos and sea turtles. We were closer to Haiti than we were to Nassau. We were a long way from Florida. Other than the birds and the turtles, there wasn't much to see. I felt like Columbus exploring the new world here. I hoped that the world was indeed round, and we wouldn't fall off the edge.

Our upcoming leg to Luperon would be a very long one. The waters along the route can be treacherous, at times. We had to wait for calm weather, and we could use a few supplies. We walked into Mathew Town to see what we could see. We came upon a lime green, stone-built house two blocks from the sea. It had a sign that said Cozy Corner. Inside we found a friendly bar where the gossip was flowing as fast as the beer. Everything on the menu was fried.

Our server was delightful, if not a little nosy. She asked question after question about our travels and our plans. I slipped up. When I said we were bound for Luperon, she asked if I had checked out of the Bahamas yet. There was no official Customs on the island, but the local police would sign the paperwork. I didn't have any paperwork. We had never officially checked in. Yolanda didn't even have a passport. I hoped that the waitress had a little pirate in her. I put my finger over my mouth, and gave her the "mum's the word" signal.

Her veins contained no pirate blood, apparently. In short order a local policeman was standing by our table, clearing his throat. He was in his seventies and more frail than Barney Fife. His uniform was a few sizes too big, and wrinkled. He carried no weapon, not even a Billie club.

"Please present your travel documents," he said.

He removed his hat and held it with both hands in front of his belt buckle. He tried to stand up a little straighter.

"I'm sorry, sir," I said. "They are on our boat. We anchored off your docks. Didn't know there was a customs procedure here."

"It is informal, sir," he said. "But we do have rules in the Bahamas. If you fail to check out here, you must return to Mayaguana for official departure papers."

"We are indeed going to Mayaguana," I lied.

"Very well," he said. "Sorry to disturb your meal."

He gave the evil eye to our waitress. I gave the evil eye to our waitress. We couldn't dawdle here. Someone more official would show up eventually. Once we pulled anchor, they wouldn't know if we went to Mayaguana or not. The way the folks in here were gossiping, everyone in the place probably knew our names and destination by now. Such is the life of an outlaw. It got tiring sometimes, dodging the law. Even in this remote outpost, my past hindered me.

"Are we okay?" asked Yolanda.

"It's fine," I said. "The old codger is mad that our waitress disturbed him, but we can't stay."

I stiffed our server on the tip, and we returned to the boat. I was going over the charts and trying to get some weather information when Yolanda brought me a cup of coffee.

"We cannot run forever, Breeze," she said.

"It's what I do best," I said. "Stick with what you're good at, Dad always said."

"I am having a wonderful time, my captain," she said. "You've shown me a world I didn't know existed. I forgot the bad things, but here, even in this place, there is trouble. Someday you will be caught."

"First things first," I answered. "We get the money, then, we figure something out. The money will give us a lot more options."

"It is your money," she said. "It is not for me. What will I do, Breeze?"

I didn't have an answer. I had gotten caught up in our cruise, enjoying myself. I was enjoying being with her, even without a sexual relationship. Now I felt guilty for not considering her predicament. She was a woman without a country, but I couldn't keep her in my world. She deserved better than a drug-running fugitive from justice. She deserved better than trawler trash. In America, she could make a fresh start. I had to get her back to the states and get her set up with something. First, I had to get my money.

"We'll figure it out together, Yolanda," I said. "Now get some rest. We leave for Luperon in the morning."

Finding Andi

It was nearly two hundred miles from Mathew town, at the southwest corner of Great Inagua, to the entrance of Luperon Harbor. We'd be exposed to the fickle elements for over thirty hours. The last time I set out on a voyage without proper weather information, I'd run into the teeth of a hurricane. On my last trip through the Bahamas, I'd almost capsized *Ashes Aweigh*, and terrified both Andi and myself, because I'd half-assed my weather research. For someone who prided themselves on seamanship, I'd pulled some dumb moves.

Now I was jumping off into dangerous waters, with no idea what lie ahead, weather-wise. We'd gotten lucky while taking the Great Iguana route. The guide books all warn about slogging directly into the eye of the trades. We had to buck the mainstream of the Equatorial Current, but the winds had been almost nonexistent. I was really pushing my luck now. I was in a hurry. I could smell the fertile soil of the Dominican. I could smell my money.

We kept our eye on the skies as we crossed, but saw nothing alarming. I used the time to consider how to handle the Commandancia once we got to Luperon. I wasn't really welcome there anymore. On my first visit, I'd bribed the man who oversaw the harbor. He stamped my passport, but looked the other way concerning my status. When I returned on my way back from the BVI's, he'd run me out of town. The American embassy had been made aware of my visit, and asked that I be detained if I ever returned. The Commandancia didn't have me arrested, but made me leave immediately.

That was over a year ago. Maybe I could get in and out before anyone raised a fuss. Either Andi gave me the money or she didn't. There was no reason to hang around for long. Maybe I could bribe him again.

I couldn't sneak in after dark. Local fishermen strung fishing nets across the entrance at night. I'd have to deal with the man, see what happened.

Our crossing was relatively uneventful. My luck had held out. It got pretty rough, but never dangerous. Yolanda didn't seem bothered by the heavy seas. They didn't bother me, but I was beginning to worry about the state of my vessel. Leap of Faith desperately needed an oil change and regular maintenance. Luperon was a great place to do it, if they let us stay.

We finally found the harbor entrance during the afternoon of the second day. I asked Yolanda to pretty herself before we dropped anchor. Her beauty might help smooth things over. Andi's presence had certainly helped on my first visit. The winter cruising season was over, so the harbor wasn't crowded. I picked a good spot, set the hook, and waited for customs officials to arrive. They wouldn't be on alert. When I was here before, I was aboard *Ashes Aweigh*. *Leap of Faith* was a stranger to them.

The local authorities wasted no time. The small boat pulled alongside almost immediately. The Commandancia stood with his arms crossed, looking serious. He recognized me immediately.

"I am surprised to see you again," he said. "Have the problems with your passport been resolved?"

"They have not," I answered. "My vessel is in need of attention. I seek safe harbor to affect repairs. I'll be in and out as quickly as possible. I also have a passenger. She is a Cuban refugee. Neither of us can meet your Customs requirements."

I was at his mercy. He put one hand under his chin to think it over. Yolanda came to my side. The Commandancia saw her and smiled.

"You bring such beautiful ladies to our harbor," he said. "How can I say no to you, Breeze?"

"Is Andrea Mongeon here?" I asked.

"She is indeed," he replied. "Thank you for introducing her to our humble home. She has improved our lives simply with her presence. She has opened a clinic in town as well."

We were off to a great start. We could stay, and Andi was here. I invited the men aboard for refreshments. Yolanda had poured cold sodas for the men, and a spread of cheese and crackers was arranged on the salon table. The Commandancia explained that Andi had flown into town like a whirlwind. Her clinic was a multi-purpose, social working, benefit to the locals. She cleaned the children's teeth and took care of minor medical problems. She secured books, paper, and pencils for the school, offering tutoring services. She would canvas the neighborhoods to determine their needs. Then she would fulfill them as best she could. She provided new blankets, new clothes and shoes to the needy. She had earned the status of a saint. Everyone loved her.

I guessed that some of my money had birthed this venture of hers. At least it was being put to good use. I couldn't wait to see her. What would she say? How would it turn out?

"I would like to visit with her tomorrow," I said.

"As always, I do not wish to know your personal affairs," he said. "But, will she be pleased to see you?"

"I don't know," I answered truthfully. "But I will not cause trouble for you, either way."

"Yes, very good," he said. "You keep your head down while you are here. Fix your boat quickly and go, before anyone asks any questions."

We shook hands and the men departed. Tomorrow, I would know. Yolanda and I were both worn out, so we rested. That evening we sat on deck to watch the sun set over the high hills. The harbor was surrounded by mountainous terrain. It was lush and green, wet with dew and rain. The soil here was rich and pungent. It stained the harbor after each rain, turning it into coffee. Boats flushed overboard, further fouling the waters. Amenities were primitive, but cheap. Diesel fuel was hauled out to you in drums, which were then pumped into your tanks from small boats.

"What will we do when this is over?" asked Yolanda.

It wasn't the first time she had asked, and I still didn't have an answer. I'd stayed focused on this mission. The money gave me tunnel vision. Still, I had to do something for this girl.

"What would you like to do?" I asked.

"I must go to America," she said. "Only there can I attain legal status. No other country will allow me."

"Then that much is settled," I said. "We'll go back to the states."

"Where will we go?" she asked.

"Not the Keys," I said. "Miami is not so good either. Didn't you say there were relatives in Baltimore?"

"Cousins on my father's side," she said. "Maria and Elena Aldama. They were born in America. I have never met them, just heard stories."

"We could try to find them," I said. "Can't be too many Aldamas in Baltimore."

She shrugged, so I explained about phone directories, computers and Google. Hell, we could probably find them on Facebook. We agreed that once my business with Andi was finished, we would start looking for her cousins.

The sun rose the next morning with a sparkling brilliance. Today was the day. I rushed Yolanda to get ready, impatient to have my showdown. We tied the dinghy off and walked the dusty street into town. I found Andi's place. It had been painted in bright, Caribbean colors. There were flower boxes under the windows. The blooms added to the explosion of color the little building threw off. It glowed like a shining beacon amongst the brown rust and gray concrete of its neighboring shacks.

I sat Yolanda on a bench just outside the door and went inside alone. Andi had her back to me, but turned when I entered. Her eyes flashed fear, but quickly softened. Once again, I was taken aback by her stunning beauty. I had seen her face a thousand times, but it still gave me butterflies to look at her.

"Did you miss me?" she said. "Or are you here about the money?"

"To which money do you refer?" I asked.

She looked puzzled, but answered right away.

"The money I took when I left you in the BVI," she said. "I still have most of it. You can have it back. I secretly wished that you would come for it."

"How did you expect I'd ever find you," I asked.

"Well, you did, didn't you?" she answered. "You are a very resourceful man, Breeze."

"You don't know what I've been through to get here," I told her.

"And the girl?" she said, pointing her chin out the window at Yolanda. "Are you lovers?"

"She is too young and pretty for an old boat bum like me," I said. "More like my little sister."

"You underestimate yourself, Breeze," she said. "You have a certain charm. Any woman who got to know you, would find you irresistible. I certainly did."

She did that finger in her hair, twirling thing. It was something a teenage girl would do. She put her head down, turning her eyes up to look at me. It was her signature move and it worked every time. She was trying to soften me up.

"I'm not after that money," I said. "You keep it. This is great what you're doing here."

"Then what exactly are you talking about?" she asked.

"Andi, the Grand Banks has been sold. That idiot Miami broker says he wired the money to you, as the legal owner. I'm here for that money. Six hundred thousand dollars."

"Oh Breeze," she said. "I had no idea. To what account?"

"I don't know," I said. "The one you wrote the check on, I suppose."

"I swear. I haven't touched that account since I left the states," she said. "I all but drained it when I left. It's not like I get bank statements in the mail here."

"Can you check?" I pleaded.

"Certainly, we'll have to go down to the café," she said.

"I'd like to go right now," I said.

She grabbed a laptop and off we went. She introduced herself to Yolanda, and they exchanged pleasantries. They were being polite, but they were sizing each other up. I could see it in their eyes. Andi was examining her younger counterpart, taking her measure. Yolanda was inspecting my ex-lover, deciding if she was worthy. Finally, they shook hands and traded "nice to meet you."

I looked over Andi's shoulder as she opened her laptop. I wanted to see for myself. The connection was slow, and several agonizing minutes went by. Her account summary appeared. There it was. She had six hundred thousand, eighteen dollars and twenty-one cents in her account.

"My God," she said. "I'm so sorry, Breeze. I really didn't know about this. I know what you must think of me, but I would never knowingly take this money. It's yours."

"It will be mine when I have it in my hands," I said. "I don't know what you have to do, to get it to me, but please hurry. The Commandancia won't let me stay for long."

"I will, Breeze. I will. Please don't hate me for this. I didn't know. I swear."

She went off to the bank to look into recovering those funds. Yolanda and I killed time by walking the streets of the town. After a few blocks, we came upon a small Catholic chapel. I asked her to wait outside, as I entered. It was a simple church, but very clean and bright. It was not overly ornate like the Catholic churches I had seen in America. There was one stained-glass window above the cross that allowed colored light to shine on the podium.

I've never been much of a religious man, but the quiet beauty of this house of God humbled me. I knelt at the altar. I bowed my head and closed my eyes. I thanked God. I thanked him for our safe passage. I thanked him for bringing Yolanda into my life. I thanked him for the money I was about to receive. I could have confessed my sins. I could have asked for guidance, but I did neither. I simply gave thanks.

When I finished the priest was standing over me. He made the sign of the cross, and said, "Amen."

"Thank you, father," I said. Then I reached into my pocket and handed him a hundred dollar bill.

"Alms for my forgiveness," I said.

"You are troubled," he said. "But, you did not ask God for help."

"God helps those who help themselves," I said.

He nodded in understanding.

I sat on a bench outside while Yolanda went in to pray. While I waited, my thoughts returned to the future. My conscience had been nagging me since I first thought I'd get the money. A little angel appeared on my shoulder to offer guidance. I could go straight, it told me. I could use the money to repay what I stole. I could hire a lawyer, and settle up with the IRS. Once I was no longer a wanted man, I could get a job. I could settle into a normal, middle-class lifestyle like society demanded.

Before I could think that through, a little devil appeared on my other shoulder. "Screw that," he said. I chuckled to myself. I was surprised the little devil had made an appearance so close to a church. He told me that I could live large on the six hundred grand. I could get some fake documents and change my identity. I should find a tropical spot to waste away my days drinking umbrella drinks. The Caribbean was full of guys like me. It was a sunny spot for shady people.

I snapped out of it when Yolanda came out of the church. We were to meet Andi at Papo's Restaurant. Her shop was on Indepencia. The restaurant was on Duarte, back towards the docks and one block over. We walked past the market, the general store, and the courthouse. Each of the locals we met had a big smile and a hearty "good afternoon" for us. This place may have lacked sophistication, but it was not uncivilized.

When Andi arrived, she was smiling too. She had good news. Although the local bank could not produce the necessary cash to accept transfer of my funds, a sister branch in Santiago could handle the transaction. I'd have my money in forty-eight hours. I gave her a big hug. I gave Yolanda a hug. We all hugged together, which made me think of a threesome. Wouldn't that be something? I ordered all of us the most expensive meal on the menu, which cost about eight bucks, American.

"What will you do now?" asked Andi.

"First, I have to get Yolanda into America, again," I answered.

"After that?" she said.

"I'm still working that out," I told her.

"You should buy your way out of trouble, Breeze," she said. "You can't run forever."

First it was the little angel, and now it was Andi, urging me to make amends. I turned to look at Yolanda.

"She's right," she said. "I know that you are a good man. You must do what is right."

"Let's get you taken care of first," I said. "Then I'll worry about me."

Before we parted, I asked Andi if she would take Yolanda shopping. I wanted her to get some nice clothes, and a real bikini or two. I figured Andi could talk her into something a little sexier than the one she had. Tomorrow I'd work on the boat, while the two of them had a girl day. I was sure that Yolanda had to be tired of being cooped up on a boat with me, and *Leap of Faith* desperately needed my full attention. I had two days to get her squared away. I could also use those two days to think, without the judgment of two pretty women and an angel.

The next day, I walked with Yolanda to meet Andi. I mentioned the two Cuban-American cousins, and asked if she could look them up on Facebook. I stopped in to see Lenin Fernandez at the marina. He had everything I needed to work on the boat.

First I changed the oil. It was thin and very black, indicating that an oil change was way overdue. I replaced the oil filter, then both fuel filters. I managed to make a huge mess while changing the oil in the injector pump. I dropped the funnel and watched helplessly as a quart of nasty oil drained into the bilge. I cursed for a minute, and then I remembered where I was. It was no big deal to pump dirty bilges into the harbor here. In fact, it was standard procedure. I pumped the glop overboard and mopped up what remained on the bilge floor. By the time I was finished I was covered in oil and sweat, but it felt good. This was a bonding time for me and *Miss Leap*. I was showing her that I cared about her.

I tightened up the belts, checked the through-hulls, and hydrated the batteries. I crawled around in the engine compartment, looking for corrosion or drips. I check the rate of flow from the stuffing box, and snugged it up just a bit. I spent all afternoon lubricating the things that move, and tightening the things that didn't.

Satisfied with my efforts, I decided I deserved a beer. As I opened the refrigerator, the little container of Laura's ashes caught my eye. I hadn't spoken to her since the Bald Mark encounter. I started to feel guilty, but washed it away with a long, cold drink of beer. I took her out on deck with me.

"Looks like I'll be in the money soon," I said. "I suppose I should ask your opinion too."

She didn't respond. I knew that she would agree with the girls, but I imagined otherwise. I pretended that she was telling me to stay on the boat. *Leap of Faith* was her home now. I had to keep the boat always, for her. I put my feet up and lay back in the afternoon sun. I closed my eyes and heard her voice in my mind.

"Whatever you decide, Breeze, as long as we're together."

I fell asleep, and slept until it was time to meet my two lady friends. They were both excited and giggling. Yolanda had two bags of clothes. She had sundresses, sandals, and yes, she had bikinis. She blushed when she showed them to me. I couldn't wait to see her wear them. Andi winked at me. Even better, they had found Yolanda's cousins on Facebook. Friend requests had been sent, along with messages explaining who she was. Hopefully, one or both would respond soon.

It looked to me that the two girls had become fast friends. I wondered how much they had shared about me. I'd find out soon enough. We took Andi back to the boat with us. As Yolanda prepared dinner, Andi confided in me.

"That girl is crazy about you, Breeze," she said. "She worships the ground you walk on. Or in your case, the deck you walk on."

"She's never given me a hint," I said. "Plus, I'm too old for her."

"You freed her from Cuba. You rescued her from a rapist. You risked your life for her. You're her hero. She also thinks you're handsome. You'd make a fine couple, and I'd be jealous."

"Just because I fantasize about having sex with her, it doesn't mean I want to be with her forever," I said. "With my luck, she'd have me stuck in a job I hated. She'd start spitting out babies, getting fatter with each one."

"You're awful, Breeze," said Andi. "Won't you ever just love someone?"

"I did once," I said. "You know that."

Andi had tried her best to win my heart. She was everything any man could ever hope for. She had offered herself to me, and I failed to accept. The spot inside me that could really, truly love, was still inhabited by Laura. Spreading Laura's ashes had freed me of my guilt. It had opened me to the possibility of a new relationship someday. I was getting laid now, whenever the opportunity arose. I had not fallen in love, not with Andi, not with Yolanda.

"You do right by her," said Andi. "Don't screw her up. I'm still trying to get my head on straight after leaving you."

"I'm sorry," I said. "I'll do my best. I promise."

Yolanda brought our dinner to us. We all sat and talked and watched the sun go down. I ruined my beautiful evening by pondering my stupidity. What the hell was wrong with me? Here I sat with two gorgeous women, either of whom would make love to me if I asked, and I would go to bed alone. That would come with obligations, the kind I simply couldn't keep. My body was screaming for fulfillment. My mind was saying NO. It was all I could do to keep from saying out loud, "Who wants to sleep with me tonight?"

I decided to think about money instead, and what I would do with it. A naked image of Yolanda snuck into my head. Could the money help me to make a life with her? An image of Andi naked crept in. She and I could have a great life together. My mind was in turmoil, so I dismissed it all. I needed rum. When in doubt, drink rum. It helped me to sleep. I didn't think about either woman that night. I didn't think about Laura either. I dreamt of steering *Leap of Faith* on the high seas. I dreamt that the Great and Mighty Breeze ruled a watery world full of danger and excitement.

The next morning I didn't even rule my own boat. Both of my girl friends were already up. The coffee was ready and breakfast was cooking.

"It's about time you got up," said Andi. "We could have set off a bomb in here last night and you would have never heard it."

"What did you two do after I went to bed?" I asked.

"Wouldn't you like to know," she answered. "We found ways to entertain ourselves."

Was Yolanda blushing? Did this entertainment take place in bed? *Great Breeze. Every man's fantasy is taking place in the next room and you're passed out in a rum haze. Could have had that threesome if you'd have played your cards right.* The picture of the two of them naked together entered my mind and wouldn't leave. Andi was a skilled lover with plenty of experience. She was a worldly woman. As far as I knew, Yolanda was a virgin. She kept her back to me as she scrambled eggs at the galley stove. I gave Andi a questioning look. She winked at me.

"Wash up and eat your breakfast," she said. "We're going into town to check Facebook. I'm going to set up an account for Yolanda, so she can communicate directly with her cousins if they respond."

"Good idea," I said. "I'll finish up getting the boat ready. Tell her to never reveal our location, okay?"

"Ah, yes," she said. "Life with Breeze. Always on the run."

"I seem to recall that you didn't mind it so much," I said.

"It was lovely," she said. "Every day was wonderful, and I'd do it again if you would have me."

"Let's not go there," I said. "I have enough on my plate with Yolanda."

"Meade Edwin Breeze," she said. "You could have so much more with either of us. What is it about you? How does a guy like you end up in paradise, with not one, but two attractive women vying for his attention?"

"Just lucky I guess."

"And not smart enough to realize just how lucky he is," said Andi.

That last comment hit me in the face like a bucket of ice water. Maybe she was right. The smart thing to do would be forget about Laura, forget about true love. Andi and I knew each other intimately. We could have a fine life together. Yolanda idolized me apparently. She was young and pretty and vaguely exotic. I could be happy with her too. I had a fine boat. I would soon be reasonably wealthy, from my perspective. I could live in some tropical paradise with the lady of my choice. I really was lucky. So why wasn't I jumping at the chance?

"You're right," I said. "I'll give it some thought. I've been running for so long now, I didn't see it. Forgot how to just be happy, I guess. Thank you for everything."

Cashing In

Our Cuban connections in Baltimore responded with enthusiasm. They were willing to help in any way they could. Yolanda was delighted. Family is very important in Cuban culture. You often see several generations of extended family living together in one house. Now, Yolanda had a place to go, where she would be accepted. I just needed to get her there. Maryland was a very long way from Luperon.

I knew the waters of the Chesapeake Bay very well. I had grown up there, fishing the bay from the Choptank River to the Susquehanna Flats. I'd even been to Baltimore by boat, many years ago. My daughter still lived in the area, somewhere in Middletown, Delaware. She had a restaurant on the

C & D Canal that was part of a marina. I'd have to be careful, to avoid the law, but I could sneak in for a visit once we made it to the Chesapeake. The plan was all coming together. First I needed to get the money.

I was concerned about Andi traveling back from Santiago with all that cash, but she had enlisted Willie Soto to escort her. He acted as a sort of constable in the town, and would be armed. Yolanda would tag along with them, while I finished preparing the boat for travel. I had a hard time concentrating that day. All I could think about was getting my hands on the money. I topped off the water tanks, and had the marina boys bring me out some diesel fuel. To occupy my mind, I sat down with the charts to decide on a route to the Chesapeake Bay. I had never considering returning home. That's what I had run away from. There were warrants for my arrest. That's where Laura had died.

I thought about re-entering the states somewhere else. I could put Yolanda on a plane. Then I thought better of it. No, I would carry this through. I was responsible for her. I'd see that she made it safely to Maryland, aboard my boat. I'd try to see my daughter.

She didn't know if I was dead or alive. I'd simply disappeared one day. Thank God she was a mature adult, and could take care of herself.

The most direct route to America was to pass to the north of Cuba and make landfall in south Florida. I could not risk it. If we had trouble for some reason, I'd never get out of Cuba a second time, especially with the girl. I had traveled through the Bahamas without showing my passport before. I'd have to try it again. We'd avoid the population centers and hop the out islands. I'd fly the quarantine flag, and shun the authorities. We'd cross the Gulf Stream from Gun Cay, south of Bimini, and make landfall near Fort Lauderdale.

The boat was ready. I was ready. It would be a long trip, but we would see the islands. I pictured Yolanda on a white sand beach in one of her new bikinis. Maybe if we were all alone, on some tropical island beach, she would loosen up. Now that I knew she cared for me, things were different. I wouldn't rush her, or force her into anything. She'd have to make the first move.

It was time to meet the girls and Willie. I tied off at the dock and walked up Indepencia towards Andi's clinic. I exchanged "good afternoons" with everyone on the street. I was in a good mood. I was in a great mood. I'd waited a long time and been through a lot, to get to this day. I'd take that money, finish my mission, and ride off into the sunset. I'd be financially secure. I could finally do whatever I damn well pleased.

They were waiting for me when I arrived. With great flourish, Andi presented me with a new briefcase. I opened it to inspect the cash. Neatly stacked American bills greeted me. I just stood and stared at it for a minute, a goofy grin on my face.

"Thank you, Andi," I said. "Thank you, thank you, thank you."

"It was my pleasure," she said. "It's been good to see you again. And so nice to meet you, Yolanda."

"This will be the third time we've parted ways, Andi," I said. "Can we at least have a proper goodbye this time?"

Then she started to cry. She came to me and put her head on my chest. She put her arms around me and held me tight. I hugged her, choking back my own tears.

"You are the finest woman I know, Andrea Mae Mongeon."

"And you're a fine man, Meade Edwin Breeze. Please promise me you'll get your life straight."

"Why does it always have to be like this for us," I said, changing the subject. "The time is never right."

"Maybe someday," she said. "You know where I live."

With that we parted. Yolanda and I walked back to the docks without saying a word. When we boarded the boat, she broke the silence.

"She is a special lady for you, no?" she said. "Why don't you make a life with her?"

"I've asked myself that same question," I said. "But I really don't have a good answer. I guess I'm just supposed to be someplace else. Right now that place is Maryland. I've got to get you back to the states."

"Thank you," she said, as she touched my hand. "I wouldn't have blamed you for staying with her, or taking her with you. Most men would have chosen her."

I didn't know what to say, so I just shrugged.

"But you are not like most men," she continued. "There is something special about you."

"Nothing special about a dope-selling fugitive from justice," I said.

"I don't care about your life before," she replied. "I see what's inside you. None of that matters to me."

"Well, thanks for your faith in me," I said. "Now, let's concentrate on getting home. It may take a month or more, depending on weather. It's a long way."

"Aye, aye, captain," she said.

We left before first light to begin the eighty mile run to Big Sand Cay. I skirted the mud flats and the fishing floats as we departed the harbor and entered the big ocean. Winds were light out of the south. At seven knots the trip would last twelve hours. There was an easy anchorage on the western side of the uninhabited jewel of an island. Some of the best beachcombing in the islands could be found there. Humpback whales also paid a visit during the month of February. It was an island paradise with no people. It was just what we needed.

Just off the southern tip of Big Sand Cay lie the South Rocks. You can see them in the daylight, so I wanted to make it before dark. Endymion Rock was a little to the south and west, and was hard to spot. I had three different charts of the area and none of them agreed on the exact location. That stretch of water was best navigated during the day. We had no problems and the anchor was set in time to enjoy the sunset.

From that spot in the world, there was nothing to block our view for a thousand miles. The calm, blue expanse of sea was a mirror for the heavenly palette of colors in the sky. As the sun slipped below the horizon, it winked at us, as if we shared a secret. There was no green flash, but it was glorious nonetheless. It was downright spiritual. I hadn't felt so happy since before Laura died. I was happy at sea. The sea had sustained me since her death. Now, my boat and I played host to a lovely young woman, here in our own heavenly place. I had a fortune stowed below. Things were looking up.

The next morning things improved even more. I convinced Yolanda to stay another day so we could play on the beach. We were safe from prying eyes here and the weather was gorgeous. She came out on deck in one of her new bikinis. My eyes tried to jump out of my head and I spit my coffee out. Have you ever seen a woman who was somewhat attractive fully clothed, but transformed into a goddess in a bikini? Her body was a sight to behold. She wasn't thin enough to be a Victoria's Secret model. There was nothing bony about her. Instead she was rounded in all the right places. She was curvy and soft and I couldn't stop staring.

"You're embarrassing me," she said. "Have you never seen a woman in a bathing suit before?"

"Not one like you," I said. "You're beautiful, and you have no reason to be ashamed of your body."

She smiled and tossed a towel at me. Later, I lay down on that towel and stared up at the clouds. We played that game where you see objects, animals, or even people in the puffy white shapes. She lay next to me. Her wet body glistened in the afternoon sun. I had the strong urge to roll over and just take her, right there on the beach. Instead I resisted. We went for a walk along the shore, picking up shells. It was one of the most carefree days I'd ever experienced.

I could live like this, I thought to myself. I could find a woman closer to my age and just hang out in the islands forever. I could return to Andi, and ask her to come along with me. This was the life for me. I could stay happy in a place like this.

That night after sunset, Yolanda shared her thoughts. They were similar to mine. It was like she had read my mind.

"Why can't we just stay here forever?" she asked. "Today was wonderful."

"Indeed it was," I said. "But in America you will gain your freedom. There's a great big world out there that you've never seen. You can make your life into whatever you wish."

"It has all been like a dream to me," she said. "First I left my home country. I go to America but am forced to run. Then we are in another country and you are a rich man. Now we are here in this place. I'm afraid I will wake from this dream in my own bed, back in Cuba."

"That's not going to happen," I said. "I will see to it."

That night she came to my bed, wearing nothing. She slid under the sheets and softly stroked my face. I tried to speak but she hushed me. Her hand was slowly working its way south. I wanted to resist. Breeze junior had other ideas. He was very interested in this new development. My heart was telling me no.

"I want to do this for you," she whispered. "It is all I have to give. I owe you so much."

My little angel was screaming "NOOO!" The little devil appeared but the angel zapped him with a lightning bolt. Breeze junior was begging, "PLEASE." I couldn't do it. She was so young and innocent. I was still trawler trash. This was no life for her. I would screw it up for her, like I'd done with everything else. Her hand reached its target and she let out a little gasp. I let out a bigger one.

"How can you say no, with this?" she said. "I will be good for you. We will be good for each other."

"I'm sorry," I said. "You deserve better than me. I don't want to hurt you. You will find someone to love you, like I can't."

I couldn't believe these words were coming out of my mouth. I was so rock-hard it was painful. There she was, in all her glory, asking me to make love to her. I couldn't explain it to myself. Something in my conscience was telling me not to do it. If it was her first time, let it be with someone special, not some broken-down boat bum with no future. I would drop her off in Baltimore and never see her again. *Don't break her heart, Breeze.*

"I'm sorry," I said again. "I don't want to hurt you. I want you, but it wouldn't be right."

"You are special," she said. "I've never met a man who would say no in this situation."

"Oh, I'm sure I'll regret it," I said. "You will make someone very happy someday."

She snuggled in beside me and let out a sigh.

"Just hold me for tonight," she said. "I am safe with you."

I held her. I held her softly for a long time before I drifted off to sleep. I listened to her breathing. I could feel her heart beating next to mine. I dreamt of making soft, gentle love. The woman in my dream was Laura.

Cruising North

When I awoke the next morning, she wasn't in my bed. I could smell the coffee and hear the bacon sizzling in the galley. Yolanda stood at the stove, wearing an oversized shirt and panties. She looked as bright and fresh as the morning sun. Her long, brown hair was braided off to one side. The braid hung down in front of her shirt. I was feeling pretty stupid about turning her down, but she didn't mention it.

"Good morning, Breeze," she said. "Did you sleep well?"

"Like a rock," I answered. "All that fun in the sun wore me out."

"Will we do it again today?" she asked.

"I think we should move on," I said. "The next leg is a long one, and I don't want to stay in any one place for too long.

"You are the captain," she said.

I browsed a chart book as we ate. Our next stop would be Sapodilla Bay, at the top of the Turks and Caicos. There was a Customs and Immigration office there, but it was up over a hill on the other side of the island. I wanted to avoid Turtle Cove, on the north coast of Provo, as there was more of a chance for trouble in the bigger city. We should have left already. We'd be pushing it to arrive before dark. The Caicos Banks were nothing to trifle with in the dark.

I left the breakfast dishes for Yolanda and went to ready *Leap of Faith* for the journey. It was nice to have a woman to share some chores with. I'd been by myself for far too long. We were already underway when she joined me on the bridge. The seas were calm as we motored over the banks. The water was so clear; I could make out every detail on the bottom. Some of the coral heads and rocks looked threatening, so I steered around them. It was hard to judge just how deep or shallow they were. I didn't take any chances.

Yolanda sat quietly, reading a book. We barely spoke all day. I felt awkward about the silence, and about the previous night. She didn't seem to be bothered by it. I kept checking our estimated time of arrival, and adjusted speed accordingly. I hated to push my old boat, but we needed to pick up the pace. The engine was just over one year old, and her maintenance was now up-to-date. She could take the strain. I eased the throttle forward and listen to the diesel's song. I kept an eye on the gauges, monitoring temperature and oil pressure. All was well.

I had the autopilot engaged, so I turned to Yolanda to break the silence.

"Are you not talking to me?" I asked.

"Oh, no," she said. "I'm just engrossed in this book. Everything is fine. Wonderful, even."

She reached over and touched my arm. Her smile seemed genuine.

"I'll go make us some lunch," she said. "Then you can tell me some sea stories."

I told her how I had narrowly escaped the law one day at Fisherman's Village Marina, in Punta Gorda. A man had come down the docks looking for me. He looked like a detective. I ran to my dinghy and set out across Charlotte Harbor, only to run out of gas. Fortunately, he had no way to pursue me on the water. I rowed the rest of the way and took off for Pelican Bay.

I told her how Andi and I got caught in a storm on the way to Georgetown. I embellished the size of the waves and the force of the wind. I acted out my role, jostling back and forth on the bridge, desperately hanging on to the helm. I made wind noises and pretended waves were crashing over the bow. I called out for Poseiden to save me. Then I played Andi's role. I curled up in a ball in the corner and whimpered.

I told her the story of the purse snatchers in Fort Myers Beach. She laughed when I kicked Butch in the balls and lost a flip flop in the process. I told her about the sweat and mosquitoes and mangroves of Punta

Blanca where I brewed my homemade rum. I told her about hiding in the bushes under a poncho as a helicopter rained down insecticides.

She was a great listener. She followed intently and asked good questions.

"You have had so much adventure," she said. "You are like a dashing pirate."

"I'm just telling you the exciting stuff," I said. "Most of the time I'm bored to death. I tend to my pot plants. I sit and watch the rum still. Sometimes, I go a month without ever speaking to another human being."

"You must get lonely," she said, touching my arm again.

"It's the price I pay for being a fugitive. I have to stay on the outskirts of society to survive."

"Now you have money," she said. "You can fix this thing. No?"

"To tell you the truth," I said. "I kind of like being an outlaw. It's who I am now. It's a hard life, but it's a free life. I answer to no one. Not the law, not the IRS, not some asshole boss, no one.

Maybe I was a pirate, born two hundred years too late.

"You already know how I feel about this," she said. "You need to do what's right."

"Well, I haven't made up my mind, yet," I answered.

It was the truth. I had put off even thinking about what to do with my future. I'd gotten good at life on the lam. With the money, it would be so much easier. What if I turned myself in, and they locked me up? I couldn't stand to go to jail. It would kill me, or at least drive me insane. I put it out of my mind once again. We were nearing our destination. We'd stop for the night, and leave in the wee hours for Rum Cay. It would be another long day, but I had to skirt Mayaguana. They had flagged my passport and come after me on my last visit.

I missed the sunset. We arrived just as it was going down, and I was busy getting the anchor set. I hated to miss the sunset. We were both hungry and tired from the long trip. While Yolanda started dinner, I went to take a shower. I came out in just my boxers. I was going to sleep in them so I saw no sense in putting on fresh clothes until tomorrow. She'd seen more of me the night before, so what did it matter now? After dinner, it was her turn to shower. She came out in just her panties. I got a good look at her breasts before she put on her robe. I couldn't tell if she was teasing me, or tempting me. She had certainly gotten over her earlier modesty. We were comfortable in each other's presence now.

After a nightcap, I went to bed and thought of her. Half of me was proud for not sleeping with her. It took some will-power. It had seemed like the right thing, though. The other half regretted not partaking of her youthful ripeness. I could still change my mind. She was obviously willing. I doubted she would make another move. I'd embarrassed her once already. It would be up to me to signal my willingness, if I chose to do so.

I tried not to think of her lying naked in the next stateroom. I wondered if she was thinking about me.

I slept fitfully. My mind bounced back and forth. My thoughts moved from Yolanda to Laura to turning myself in. As nice as it was here, I missed Pelican Bay and southwest Florida. I wanted to go back there, back to life the way it was. I missed Laura too. I had conquered my grief, but she was still there. When we were together, I could always count on her counsel. Life's decisions were shared. Now I was on my own, and I'd made a mess of things. Finally I gave up. I went into the salon and picked up Laura's ashes. I took them out on deck and looked up to the night sky. Billions of stars twinkled in the clear night.

I knew it was crazy to speak to her ashes, but it was all I had left of her. I focused on the brightest star and spoke aloud.

"What do I do know?" I said. "Just give me a sign, Laura. Let me know you're watching over me."

A falling star sparked across the twinkling panorama. My spirit jumped. She was out there. She could hear me. She had given me a sign, but what did it mean? I saw a movie once starring Robin Williams. He was able to reunite with his wife in the afterlife. I thought it was ridiculous at the time. Now I was rethinking my position.

Yolanda came out on deck in her robe. Her hair was all messed up and she had her arms crossed against the evening chill.

"How long have you been watching?" I asked.

"I heard you speak," she said. "And I saw the meteorite. It is hard to believe it happened. You must have had a very special love with her."

"I feel foolish that you heard me talking to her," I said. "But that shooting star was no coincidence."

"For miracles to happen," she said. "One must believe."

"I haven't believed in much of anything since she died," I said.

"But you felt her love, Breeze. You had your time with her," she said. "All of my life I've had nothing to believe in. I only knew oppression and poverty. I never dreamt of anything better. Now, the world is in front of me, thanks to you. It is overwhelming, the possibility."

"That's why we need to stay on mission," I said. "Get you to America, start your new life."

"I can never repay you," she said. "Come what may, you will always be special to me."

Then she spun on her heels and returned to her bunk. I thought I heard her softly crying. I could have cried myself.

To America

The fair weather held for our long journey to Rum Cay. We anchored off Port Nelson, tucked inside Sumner Point. Less than one hundred people lived on this island, but it had an abundance of bars and restaurants to cater to people like us. With the binoculars, we could make out Kay's Bar, Two Sisters, Oceanview Bar and Toby's bar. They would all have to wait. I was exhausted. I decided we'd stay here, to rest a bit before moving on. I was able to quiet the dialogue in my head, and slept like Rip Van Winkle again that night.

In the morning, Yolanda was ready for the beach. She was wearing a stunning bikini, and had a beach towel draped over her shoulders. I figured one of those bars must serve breakfast, so off we went. A very friendly woman named Doloris Wilson greeted us at Kay's Bar. She was Kay's mother, and somewhat of a local historian. She gave us a brief history of her island and asked that we stop in the General Store to purchase her book, *My Rum Cay Home*.

As we ate a delightful breakfast with some delightful people, I was feeling quite pleased with myself. It was nice to be seen in the company of a pretty young lady. We had come a long way in a short time. Our relationship seemed to have found its equilibrium. Life was good today. This island was the perfect spot to wait for weather. It had some of the finest fishing, snorkeling or diving that one could hope for. There were very few people here, but everyone was nice. If the weather took a turn for the worse, this would be a good place to wait.

We walked the beach that afternoon and talked. She wanted to know all about life in America. It would be a shock to her, I knew. She had been told that everyone in America was rich. I guessed that compared to Cubans, she was right. I told her that everyone had their basic needs met, even the poorest among us. They all had cell phones and internet on some device. Everyone was obsessed with these devices and spent many hours fiddling with them. Many owned big homes with fancy cars. Life was full of frantic stimulation and distraction. It's part of what drove me away from society. This moment, two people communicating face to face, was what life should be about.

"Do I have to go?" she asked. "I could stay with you, wherever you go."

She had tugged at my heartstrings once again. I reassured her that it wasn't all bad. Once she got her green card, she could get a job and make good money of her own. Low wage workers made seven or eight dollars per hour. I told her that the average work week was forty hours. She did the math.

"I would make more in one day than I could make in two months, in Cuba," she said.

"You're English is perfect," I told her. "You might land a job paying more. Buy yourself pretty clothes and cell phones or whatever you desire. There is always enough food. There is always enough fun. We Americans take our leisure time very seriously."

"It seems so outrageous," she said. "What if I am overwhelmed?"

"You'll get used to it," I answered. "You're smart, and you're strong. You'll be fine."

"Will you stay with me for a while?" she asked. "Help me to get acquainted?"

"You have your cousins for that," I replied. "You won't need me."

She grew quiet after that. She reached out and took my hand as we continued our stroll. The color of the water matched that of the sky. We were surrounded by oceans of blue. The air we breathed was crisp and clean. Floral scents wafted down to the beach from the flora beyond the dunes. It would be hard to leave this postcard world.

Later, we showered and put on nicer clothes. I wore my new best shirt, which Andi had bought for me. Yolanda wore a flowery sundress that showed just enough of her figure to get one's attention. We had a gourmet meal at Sumner Point Marina. Chef Jon was a culinary wizard, and our hostess Allison was quite gracious. We were living large. Both the meal and the ambience were spectacular.

The next few days passed much the same. The beach and the blue water held us like a magnet. The sun shone brightly during the day. The stars twinkled like diamonds at night. The sunsets were stunning, and coincided nicely with happy hour. The troubles of the world were forgotten. There was no Bald Mark. There was no IRS. The sins of my past couldn't find me here. There was no Cuban oppression, no communism or capitalism. Our souls were warmed by the heat of the tropical sun. We had stopped talking about the future, and the past. We lived in the moment. We were one with our surroundings. Our only concerns were the ebb and flow of the tides, the direction and speed of the wind, and what shells we might find on the beach today. This felt like living to me, but it had to end. I took some time to relax. I allowed Yolanda some time to take it all in. Now we needed to continue our journey. It was very much like the last time I had traveled the Bahamas by boat. I had a mission. I had sworn to carry out my duties. I dawdled in the wonder that is the tropics along the way, but I accomplished my goal. Now it was time to refocus.

We raised anchor the next morning, bound for Calabash Bay. Twenty miles out we ran into a problem. It turned out to be a life threatening problem. I heard a buzzing sound that I'd never heard before. It was some kind of alarm, but what did it mean? Oil pressure was good. Engine temperature was fine. All the gauges were in the normal range, but the buzz persisted. I thought back to all of the improvements that had been made at the Marathon Boat Yard. I was overlooking something, or had forgotten about it. I tried to connect with my vessel. I listened to her. I felt her. Something wasn't right. She just didn't feel right.

I shut down the engine and went below to take a look. Just as I was opening the hatch to the engine room, it hit me. It was a high-water alarm. Not good. I looked down and saw water about a foot deep in the bilge. It was clear sea water. *Leap of Faith* was sinking. Sea water was coming in from somewhere, and the bilge pumps weren't working, or were overwhelmed.

I went to the main pump, which was under a hatch toward the bow, between the stateroom and the head. I opened it. The pump was not running. The float switch was submerged and not in the up position as it should have been. I reached down and lifted the float and the pump sprang to life. Some debris or crud had fouled it. When I released it, the pump continued to run. This was a good start.

The secondary pump was further aft and a little higher in the bilge. It occurred to me that the float switch on it was not functional. I knew this, but had failed to replace it, even though I had a spare. Why hadn't I taken care of it back in Luperon when I was doing the maintenance? I had just recovered a bunch of money. I had just reunited with Andi. The dynamics of the situation had made me complacent about safety. I had been surrounded by pretty women and was literally swimming in cash. Now I was about to be swimming for my life it I didn't do something quickly. I ran forward to the breaker panel. The smaller pump still worked on manual. I flipped the switch and it started running. I went out on deck and peered over the side.

Two good, strong streams of water were pouring out of the thru-hulls. I might save her yet, I thought.

I returned to the engine room to look for the source of the water. The most likely culprit was the raw water intake that fed the water pump. I lifted that hatch and ran my hand along the hose. Sure enough, it had a split running several inches along its length. I tried to close the valve on the thru-hull, but it wouldn't budge. This was yet another maintenance item I had overlooked. I screamed for Yolanda to bring tools as I held my hands over the hose in a vain attempt to stem the flow of sea water. I kept my tool bag on the bridge. It seemed like forever, but Yolanda brought it to me within a minute. I used an adjustable wrench on the end of the lever to gain some extra leverage. Like arm-wrestling a strong man, I slowly muscled the thing closed, stopping the water. We were safe for now, but we were dead in the water. We couldn't fire the engine without fixing the hose.

I sat on the edge of the hatch with my feet dangling in the bilge. Once I caught my breath, I was able to think more clearly. I had several rolls of Rescue

Tape on board. I could wrap it up tight and we could continue, but it was only a temporary fix. The pumps had cleared all of the water. I used a crappy old towel to dry off the hose and started wrapping the tape. I'd had this stuff for years and never had a use for it. I was glad to have it then. As I wrapped, I cursed myself for not taking better care of things. The sea is a harsh mistress sometimes. If you forget that, you just might pay the price, someday. This boat was my life, and I was as experienced in such matters as anyone alive. Still, I had been lax. The fun in the sun, the women, the money; all of them had distracted me. The waters of the Bahamas were no place to let your guard down. *Some great captain you are, Breeze.*

Yolanda had been silent throughout the ordeal. She gave me a look that said, what now? I looked over the charts. We couldn't just float out here in open waters. The winds had picked up to fifteen knots out of the west, so I set a course for the east side of Conception Island. We picked our way through the reefs and rocks south of Wedge Point. Then we wound our way up the coastline. I dropped the anchor between Booby Cay and the main island. I needed to think, and I needed a beer.

After a few cold ones, I came up with an idea that just might work. I scrounged around some storage lockers until I found what I needed. I had held onto some scrap pieces of PVC pipe from some forgotten project. I grabbed a length of pipe and a hacksaw and lowered myself back into the bilge. I cut the hose clean on either side of the slit. I measured the gap and cut a piece of pipe to fit. I jammed the ends of the pipe into the open ends of the hose, and tightened it up with hose clamps. It wasn't pretty. It certainly wasn't in the finest naval tradition, but it would work. I started the engine and let it run. My redneck engineering worked just fine. At the very least, I hoped it would hold until we could get someplace to buy new hose. This brought up another problem. The obvious choice was Georgetown, where a cruising boater could find anything he needed. I couldn't enter without having Customs and Immigration board the boat. I couldn't let that happen.

Back to the charts I went. After a short study I devised a plan. I'd anchor at Fowl Cay. We could load up the dinghy with some extra gas, and make the run into Georgetown Harbor without being noticed. I'd ask my old friend Captain Fred for assistance in getting a replacement hose. I tried to relax that night, but our near catastrophe had me on edge. What else had I overlooked? I couldn't think of anything, but I still couldn't sleep. I got up and poured myself a glass of rum. Worked like a charm.

The next morning we set out early. It was twenty-five miles to Santa Maria, then a few more miles into Calabash Bay. I check the temporary hose repair every half hour. The winds clocked around from the northwest, so I continued on to Salt Pond to spend the night. While we slept, the winds shifted again. We were now better protected from the northeast blow, so we made the twenty-two mile jump over to Fowl Cay.

From there it was a reasonable dinghy ride into the anchorage at Redshanks Yacht and Tennis Club. Captain Fred's seventy foot Hatteras, Incognito, rested on her anchor there. He wasn't aboard, but I found him on the beach. He was regaling the local liveaboards with a story I'd heard a dozen times already. He had a chewed up cigar in one hand, and a bottle of Perrier in the other. As we beached the dinghy, he didn't stop his tale. He started walking our way while delivering the punch line over his shoulder to the gathered onlookers.

"My God it's Breeze with another beauty," he said. "How does a scruffy old sea dog like you keep making the acquaintance of such pretty ladies?"

"It's a long story," I told him.

"I love long stories," he said.

"As long as you're the one telling them," I replied.

"I have missed your witty banter, young Breeze," he said. "Please, sit and tell us all."

So I told them about the storm that chased me into Cuban waters. I told them about talking my way out of Cuba, and leaving with Yolanda onboard. I told them about Bald Mark, and Enrique, and fleeing for Luperon. I told them about Andi and the money and about how we limped into Fowl Cay with a busted water hose.

I even told them that we needed to stay under the radar, and why.

"You should write a book," said Fred. "All of the shit that you get into would make a great read."

"If I could ever stop getting into shit, maybe I'd have the time," I said. "I've had more than my share of excitement lately."

"A modern day pirate," he said. "Living wild and living free."

"Something like that," I said. "Sorry, but we can't hang around here for long. Can you help me get another hose?"

"It won't be a problem," he answered. "Hank over at Georgetown Marina probably has just what you need."

"I'll bring the old hose over in the morning," I said. "We can ride over to Masters Harbor together."

With that business settled, we delved into some serious drinking. Captain Fred told his stories to Yolanda and whoever else would listen. When he knew

I'd heard one before, he'd give me a wink. I just let him talk. We heard about secret spy bases in the Philippines. We heard about his rescue of Imelda Marcos and her family. We heard how he bribed certain legislators to build an airport in central Florida. We heard how he testified before congress after the Lockerbie disaster. He was a good story teller. He had his audience's full attention. The more the liquor flowed, the more animated he became. It was a shame we couldn't linger. This place, although crowded in the winter months, held a certain charm.

The sun started to fade and we were forced to leave. I didn't want to run back to Fowl Cay in the dark. Once aboard *Leap of Faith*, I headed straight for bed, but Yolanda wanted to talk.

"The Bahamas makes me drunk without drinking," she said. "There is so much life everywhere we go. It's like a dream. Are you sure you won't just take me as your own? We can live like this always."

"The authorities would catch on to us eventually," I said. "It is a dream. We have to go back to the real world, in order for you to have a real future."

"But what about you?" she asked. "Will you ever have a life in the real world?"

"I'm not sure that's what I want," I answered. "Right now, it's not about me."

We said good night, and went to our respective bunks. I lie there in the dark thinking about the women in my life. What was it about Yolanda and Andi? Why couldn't I accept either one fully and unconditionally? Andi had loved me. She was beautiful and smart and caring. Something was missing between us. Yolanda adored me. She was pretty and brave and sweet. Something was missing with her too. I thought about Laura. Our love was so intimate. Laura was a very good looking girl. She was tall and thin and blonde. Men found her very attractive, but that wasn't what our relationship had been about. We shared a oneness. Our thoughts were intertwined. There was comfort in our closeness. There was never any tension between us. It was free, easy and natural. I didn't feel like that with Andi. I was somewhat intimidated by her beauty and her brains. She was probably the only woman I'd ever met who I thought was smarter than me. There was always some underlying rivalry between us, one that I always lost.

In the short time that I'd shared with Yolanda, she'd become dependent on me. I was the older, wiser, caretaker of her life. Deep down, she was a stranger to me. I enjoyed her company. I was attracted to her full, young body, but there was no real intimacy. Neither of these women could replace what I'd lost. I wished them both happiness, but they wouldn't find it with me. I found it ironic that a guy who was willing to grow and sell dope for a living, smuggle cocaine, and steal from his employer, would suddenly develop scruples when it came to the virtue of hot, sexy women. *You are one messed up dude, Breeze.*

The following morning, Fred and I procured a new hose. We shook hands and he asked if he might see me again someday.

"Who's to say, Captain Fred?" I told him. "Wherever the wind blows and sun comes up, you might find me there."

"I envy you, Breeze," he said. "You're living free, and somehow you attract the women. It must be nice to be you."

"Trust me," I said. "You wouldn't want to trade places. Take care, my friend."

The repair was simple. *Leap of Faith* was once again ready for sea. I'd managed to slip in and out of Georgetown without attracting the wrong kind of attention, but it was time to hit the trail once again. We slipped out the back door and ran the eastern side of the island up to Cave Cay. I took the Cave Cay Cut and found a deep lagoon in the middle of the island to hide in for the night. I felt safer in secluded spots without company. Yolanda seemed to take comfort in proximity to other people. After our little brush with danger, she felt safety in numbers. She didn't talk much that night. We watched the sun set in silence.

The next day we made the short run up to Sampson Cay, where we took on fuel and water. There were a host of excellent anchorages and beautiful beaches ahead of us, but I wanted to make better time. I was feeling a sense of urgency about getting Yolanda back to the states. The longer we lingered in the Bahamas, the more likely it was that something bad would happen. I returned to my mission with renewed vigor. We skipped Warderick Wells. I would have loved to show her the Exuma Cays Land and Sea Park there, but it was teaming with Bahamian Defense Force guards and even a park warden.

We motored by Hawksbill Cay, Shroud Cay, Norman's Cay and Highbourne Cay. All of these are lovely places. It was a shame to miss out on them. We were determined to put some miles under our keel, though. I decided to anchor in a cove between Allans Cay and Leaf Cay. Again, it was a secluded anchorage. We had it all to ourselves. I was hoping that the seclusion might prompt Yolanda to shed some of her clothes, but it didn't happen. She had withdrawn a little over the previous few days. She wasn't talking much, preferring to read quietly.

After we left Allans Cay, we took a course around the busy island of Nassau. It took most of the day to reach Chub Cay, where we anchored off the beach in front of a marina. At first light the next morning,

I pointed *Miss Leap* towards Gun Cay and motored hard across the Great Bahama Banks. I gave her a little extra throttle. If we could maintain seven knots or better, we'd make it before dark. The Banks were spooky to me. They were not very deep, and the water was so clear it seemed like you were about to hit the rocks below. It gave me a sensation of floating on air. The crossing went fine. We arrived on the east side of Gun Cay just as the sun was setting over the island. We were both tired from the long run, so we hit the bunks early.

When I woke, I decided to simply go around to the west side of the island and stage there for our crossing to Florida. I figured I should do some system checks and be positive that all was well down in the engine room. I spent the day tinkering and tightening. I lubed the sticky thru-hull valve and worked it back and forth. I changed out the useless float switch on the secondary bilge pump. I checked all the fluids. When I was confident she was ready, I retired to the back deck for a cold beer.

Yolanda sat in the deck chair beside me. The afternoon sun shone behind her, almost forming a halo around her head. She looked beautiful.

"Tomorrow you will be in America," I said. "Are you ready to make a whole new life?"

She bit her lower lip and thought for a moment.

"In some ways I am ready," she said. "But in others I am not. I know it is what I have to do, but I'm afraid. I don't know what to do when we get there."

"I think that you can just present yourself to any government agency," I said. "The police, Customs, the Coast Guard, they will welcome you with open arms once you step on American soil. I think they even give you some money."

"You will help me with this, no?" she asked.

"Of course, I will," I answered. "Plus, you have your cousins in Baltimore. You'll be fine."

"It's different for you, Breeze," she said. "I have never left my home, except to visit Havana occasionally. I am like a baby bird."

"Then I guess I'm nudging you out of the nest," I said. "It's time for you to fly on your own."

I gave her a fatherly pat on the back and went off to take a shower.

That night I had a bad dream. We were in her cousin's house saying goodbye. Yolanda cried hysterically and hung on to me with all her might. I was trying to leave and she was on the floor holding onto my leg. I drug her across the floor as I tried to escape her grasp. She screamed, "Don't leave me" over and over again. I opened the door in my dream, and a bright light hit me. At the same time, I awoke to see Yolanda standing in my doorway. She had turned on the light in my cabin.

"I can't sleep," she said. "Please tell me it's going to be all right."

"Come on," I said, as I crawled out of bed. "I'll make us some coffee."

I spent the rest of the night putting a positive spin on life in America. I told her about work, and money. I told her about television, shopping malls, fast food, and new cars. I told her about Little League and Girl Scouts, soccer moms and fashion models. I told her about big cities and small towns. I emphasized freedom, and the right to make your own choices. I never mentioned crime, corruption or violence. I made the U S of A sound like heaven.

"And there's a special place in our society for pretty young ladies," I said. "You'll have the world by the balls in no time."

"You make it sound so wonderful," she said. "Why did you run away, Breeze?"

I really didn't want to talk about it. I'd had my fill of self-examination on this trip.

"It's much too long of a story," I said. "Look, the sun is coming up. Let's get you to America. We'll make it stick this time, I promise."

Wet Foot/Dry Foot

The crossing from Gun Cay to Fort Lauderdale would be fifty-four miles. At seven knots it would take eight hours. We wouldn't be traveling in a straight line though. The Gulf Stream carries slow boats to the north at an alarming pace. Instead of running a GPS rum-line towards the Port Everglades Inlet, I ran a compass course that made it look like we were heading to the northern part of Biscayne Bay. I could count on a considerable northward drift, and if my calculations were correct, we'd be in Lauderdale in time for dinner.

Everything went fine. The boat was fine. Yolanda was fine. I was fine. It couldn't have been a nicer crossing. All was well, until we entered the ICW at Port Everglades. We turned to starboard and went under the

182

17th Street Causeway. New River was to port. I wasn't sure where to go at this point. We continued north, passing under the Las Olas Bridge where I saw a few mooring balls and some anchored boats. Canals branched off in all directions. Marinas shared the shoreline with multi-million dollar homes. There were several huge cruise ships docked at the port terminal. There were many high-rise condominiums and dozens of waterfront restaurants clogging the banks. The waters were churning furiously from all the comings and goings of various vessels.

We passed the Los Olas Marina, the Hall of Fame Marina, and the ridiculously large Bahia Mar Yachting Center. Bahia Mar was the fictional home of Travis McGee. I should have just taken a slip and paid a visit to the plaque still on display in the dockmaster's office, but I was still stuck in my cheapskate ways. The further north we went, the more congested things became. Water taxis darted about. Police boats were actively enforcing the slow-speed zone. Finally, I turned around. I took us back to the Los Olas bridge and dropped the hook outside the mooring field. We were in America, safe and sound.

"It is just as I feared," said Yolanda.

"What's that?" I asked.

"The buildings, the yachts, the wealth," she said. "It's like a place from the future. It's so…busy."

"I hear you," I said. "I never got used to all this. Maybe your cousins live in a quiet suburb."

"What do we do?" she asked.

"I'm not sure. I guess we go somewhere and figure out what to do next. There's got to be a library around here somewhere."

That is what we did. We found the library and did some research. It turned out that the government has Citizenship and Immigration offices spread throughout most border-states. Some are amnesty branches, including the one nearby, in Oakland Park. It was just north of Lauderdale. We took a cab to NW 31st Avenue and pulled up in front of the USCIS building. Yolanda was visibly nervous. We sat outside on a bench to gather ourselves.

"Listen," I said. "Did anyone stop us when we motored in? America doesn't care about a boat entering from offshore. We basically have open borders. Sure you're supposed to check in if you have been to a foreign country, but who is enforcing it? This isn't like in Cuba. Unless we get arrested, no one is going to stop us and ask for papers."

"I don't know what to think," she said. "I trust you to help me."

We went inside and approached the reception desk. The nice lady smiled, and welcomed Yolanda to America. There was some paperwork to fill out. She asked if Yolanda needed any assistance with employment, childcare, medical services and so on. We explained that she had family in Maryland. The lady told us that an interview would be scheduled within a few weeks. If all went well, Yolanda would be granted temporary legal status. After one year, she could apply for a green card. In five years, she could apply for citizenship. We didn't want to hang around in Lauderdale for two weeks, so we asked for an office near Baltimore. A quick checked revealed that the closest office was in Arlington, Virginia. I said that would be fine. We gave her the address of Yolanda's relatives. That was it. She was free to move about the country. It was all too simple.

I had long been torn about American policies towards Cuba. The situation between our two nations had confounded politicians from Kennedy to Obama. Jimmy Carter had made a mess out of the Mariel Boat lift. Meanwhile, the people of Cuba still lived under an oppressive dictatorship. The Communist Party came first. The Cuban citizen came last. In south Florida, especially in the Keys, there was a strong bond with the Cuban people. The vast majority of Cuban immigrants I had met in my travels were honest, hardworking people. They were just trying to feed their families and make their way in the world like anyone else. Those still living in Cuba had no such opportunity. Some folks cheered when a boatload of refugees made it to the beach. Others wanted them sent back. The embargo had done nothing to change the lives of ordinary Cubans, but lifting it promised to only enrich the Castros. No concessions were offered concerning human rights or Democracy. In fact, Raul was now making demands of the United States. He wanted reparations for the economic hardship we had created via the embargo. He wanted us to return ownership of Guantanamo Bay. The situation was still a mess, as far as I was concerned. It seemed to me, that our government could find a better way to actually help the people of Cuba. I didn't have the answers, but I wasn't in charge.

Meanwhile, I was the steward of one certain refugee. The politics didn't matter when it came to Yolanda. All I wanted was to secure a better life for her. Wet foot/dry foot was her salvation. I had gotten her to America. I had endangered her life in the process, and my own, but we made it. This called for a celebration. We had two weeks to get to Virginia, which was pushing it, but I'd figure out the logistics later. That night we partied.

We took the dinghy down a canal that was just north of the Southeast 17th Street Causeway. We passed the Boathouse of Fort Lauderdale and admired all the shiny new yachts. At the end of the canal we found the Southport Raw Bar. After one drink, we made an easy walk down Cordova Road to the Harbor Shops.

We bought nicer clothes for an evening out. We returned to the Raw Bar's main dining room and ordered champagne. I offered a toast.

"Here's to dry feet," I said, raising my glass. "May you find happiness in your new home."

"I wish you happiness in return, Breeze," said Yolanda.

We laughed, and drank, and ate fine food for hours. Yolanda's spirits were high. I felt a huge weight had been lifted off my shoulders. We were a long way from Cuban dictators or cocaine kingpins. I had forgotten all about my own troubles with the law. I was feeling quite proud of myself. The glow didn't last long. It started to wear off as we rode back through all the high-rise buildings and commercial development. I knew this place was foreign to Yolanda, but it was foreign to me too. I didn't belong here. I belonged in the quiet, mangrove surrounded waters of Pelican Bay.

That night I worried about Yolanda's future. I was about to turn her loose into a society that I found repulsive. Soon, she'd be watching reality TV. She'd be addicted to her smart phone and shallow pursuits.

She would be swallowed up by consumerism. Her innocence would be lost, along with her dignity. She would join the trampling herd of sheep on the nine-to-five treadmill of American society, always wanting more. I supposed it was better than what she had fled, but I felt sorry about it. I could only hope that she wouldn't lose her true self. I certainly couldn't spend the rest of my life regretting what I'd done for her.

We worked our way north through Florida. We motored by Palm Beach, Fort Pierce, Vero Beach, New Smyrna and Daytona. Each day I attempted to tutor her on the ways of our society. They were long days. We had no time to waste if we wanted to reach Virginia in time for her interview with Customs and Immigration. We ran seventy miles or more each day, using up every hour of daylight. We'd anchor each night wherever we could find a likely spot. Sometimes it meant just pulling off the main waterway a few hundred feet. We passed through Jacksonville and Fernandina Beach, and then we entered Georgia.

The waterway became less cluttered, until we neared Savannah. One-eyed Al lived here, as well as my old friend Captain Carl. Carl ran one of those dinner cruise boats that plied the Savannah River. There was no time to stop and look them up. We trudged on. The days dragged on, growing longer and longer. My sermons grew longer too. There wasn't much to do sitting at the helm all day, so I preached the gospel of Breeze to Yolanda. I warned her of the dangers of submersing herself in modern American culture. I told her that I admired the person I knew, and I didn't want her to change, not too much anyway.

She grew impatient with me. She just wanted to get on with her life. She wanted to experience all that America had to offer. Somewhere around Beaufort, North Carolina, I stopped lecturing her. As we passed out of South Carolina and into Virginia, I could feel her excitement building. She started asking a lot of questions. She quizzed me on daily life. She wanted to know what people did. How does employment work? She asked me about money and banks. She asked about cars and leisure time. She asked about clothes and shoes and furniture and all the things that ordinary people concerned themselves with.

I did my best, but I warned her that I wasn't a good example of a typical American. I had shunned all of the things that most people took for granted. This concept confused her. She couldn't understand why I had dropped out of society, if it was so great. It was a hard question for me to answer. I went and got Laura's ashes and set them down on the dash.

"Something is broken inside of me," I said. "After Laura died, I couldn't see the point of it all. Going to work, buying stuff I didn't need, pretending that it all meant something; I couldn't make myself play the game anymore."

"Is she why you wouldn't make love to me?" she asked.

"Yes, and no," I answered. "If I didn't care about you, I would have done it. The thing is, I do care about you. Sex would only spoil it. We won't be spending our lives together. Cheap sex is not worth ruining our relationship. If we had just passed in the night, met in some bar, I would have been all over you. I would have known that I'd never see you again, and it wouldn't have mattered to me. I'm sorry if that sounds crude."

"I think I understand," she said. "There is much more to you than meets the eye. I hope that someday, you will resolve your inner troubles."

"I don't even know where to start," I told her. "So far I've just run away from them."

"You can't run forever," she said.

"You're not the first person to tell me that," I replied. "But for now, I'm comfortable with it. I've gotten damn good at it."

Delmarva

We left the protected waters of the ICW at Norfolk. The lower end of the Chesapeake Bay was big water, and it was open to the Atlantic Ocean. We could see the Bay Bridge Tunnel off to our east, terminating at Cape Charles on Virginia's eastern shore. The Navy yards were to our west.

I had serious reservations about returning to my home waters. The Chesapeake Bay had been my home for forty years. I was intimately familiar with its upper portions, but here, I was lost. I had fished the bridge/tunnel a few times. G-man and I had jigged the pilings for rockfish in the winter months. Cruising *Leap of Faith* on the Virginia mainland side was much different. This was the first time she had ever left the warm waters of Florida and the Caribbean. It didn't feel right, but I had a job to do. I still hoped to see my daughter while I was in the neighborhood as well.

I made a beeline for Point Lookout, at the entrance to the Potomac River. It was a long trip upriver to Washington D.C., and Arlington. I hated D.C. by car, and had never been there by boat. I called ahead to reserve a slip at Columbia Island Marina. It was on Pentagon Lagoon, just off the George Washington Memorial Parkway. Eventually, we found it, just north of the 14th Street Bridge. It was surprisingly affordable. They charged me fifty-four dollars, plus five dollars for electricity.

We took a cab to the Immigration office in Arlington. As soon as they saw Yolanda, everything was fast-tracked. Cubans get special treatment during immigration proceedings. It was apparent that this particular office didn't see many Cubans. They seemed thrilled to process the paperwork, and asked Yolanda lots of questions about her homeland. Again, it was too smooth. Just fill out this form, sign here, and you're good to go. We left with temporary legal status for Yolanda, and all the documents to prove it.

It should have been cause for another celebration, but we were both too tired to play. Two weeks of motoring all day long had worn us down. I asked Yolanda if she wanted to stay and see the Capitol, but she said no. She just wanted to get to Baltimore. It wasn't far, and I knew the way. Her ordeal would soon be over. We'd soon have to say goodbye. With that realization, we both became subdued.

After exiting the Potomac, we rounded Point Lookout and turned north towards Point No Point. I was uncomfortable on the western side of the bay, so I veered east towards Hooper Island. The eastern shore of Maryland was more to my liking. Sleepy little fishing villages still dotted the landscape, like Taylor's Island, and Tilghman Island at the mouth of the Choptank River. Beyond the Choptank, were Poplar Island and the entrance to Eastern Bay. I had fished this area hundreds of times. I knew every oyster bar, hump, and drop-off within twenty miles. It was familiar, yet it didn't feel like home anymore. We spent the night anchored off Thomas Point, at the southernmost end of Kent Island.

"Why is the water so dark?" asked Yolanda. "It's brown."

I chuckled at the question. The waters around Cuba were sapphire blue and clear down to thirty feet. The Florida Keys had some beautiful water too. Here, in the Chesapeake, the water was murky and thick. It was disgusting compared to the tropics. I never realized how bad it actually was when I lived here. Now it seemed like a muddy, stinking, puddle of pollution.

"There are multiple causes," I said. "All of the rivers bring down soil and fertilizers. The municipalities spill sewage. Chicken poop is spread on the fields. Silt pours over the dam on the Susquehanna River. It's a mess, I know."

I had no need to apologize for what the people of the region had done to this body of water. Year after year, politicians ran for office promising to **Save the Bay**. The Chesapeake Bay Foundation raised millions to increase awareness. Laws were passed. Sewage was taxed. Farmers were regulated. Still, the health of the bay declined. It was overfished, overused, and over-polluted. It could only take so much. Now it appeared to be dying. I couldn't wait to get back to Florida, which had its own problems, but nothing like this.

We shared a silent sunset.

The next morning, while we ate breakfast, I could sense something was wrong. Yolanda was fidgety and nervous. She spilled coffee down the front of her white blouse. As she looked down at the ugly stain, she began to cry. I hated it when women cried.

"Oh Breeze, I am so afraid. My new life is right here in front of me, but I feel frozen. Can't we wait another day? I'm not ready to leave you. I will never see you again. Please?"

I was feeling a bit sad about going our separate ways myself. I hadn't told her that. I had only encouraged her to look forward to life in America. One more day wouldn't hurt, I decided. Less than twenty-five miles up the eastern shore lay one of my old haunts. Rock Hall, Maryland, had once been a thriving fishing community. Everyone was a waterman. Striped bass, blue crabs, oysters and clams supported the hardscrabble families of the town. It had been a lawless place once. Men worked hard and drank harder. Scratching out a living from the bay made for tough hides. Fights were common in the waterfront bars. Taxes were avoided. Fisheries laws were ignored. The core families of the area had worked these waters for generations, but times were changing.

The oyster fishery collapsed. Stocks fell to two percent of their historic levels. Clams disappeared. Power dredging had wiped out the beds in a few short years. The watermen turned to crabbing, and soon the bay was a giant minefield of crab pot floats. All that pressure sent the crab population into a downward spiral. Hardier stock took to netting rockfish in the winter months. Poaching was rampant. Soon the fish started to disappear too.

Mortgages went unpaid. Pickup trucks were repossessed. Workboats fell into disrepair. Wealthy city dwellers started buying up the watermen's homes. Some were refurbished, but most were torn down, and replaced with modern structures. Outsiders became known as "chicken-neckers". The clash of cultures was always present. Transplants from urban areas didn't appreciate the dirty, hard men, who smelled like fish. Rusted out trucks, filled with rotting bushel baskets, were parked next to Volvos and BMWs. It was a rocky transition, but the interlopers won out in the end. Rock Hall was now a bedroom town for former residents of Baltimore, Washington, and Philadelphia.

There were a few hardcore outlaws still hanging on, but the town had been gentrified. Fancy sailboats now far outnumbered the workboats. The men who couldn't leave the water, turned to charter fishing. They could still make somewhat of a living, taking those chicken-neckers out to chase the few rockfish that remained. Even the president of the Waterman's Association was now running a charter boat. I ran charters out of the harbor myself for a time. I had fond memories of Rock Hall. That's where I decided to spend our last day together. It was directly across the bay from Baltimore.

We rounded Thomas Point light and turned north. As we motored up the shoreline of Kent Island, I thought back to all the good times I'd had in this neighborhood. Laura and I had married at the Jetty Dock Bar, in Kent Narrows. We'd listened to our favorite music at Big Owl's Tiki Bar. We could have run across Eastern Bay and docked for lunch, but I was afraid the memories would hurt.

We cruised under the Bay Bridge and up beyond Love Point. I'd hooked my biggest rockfish ever just off the LP buoy while trolling one day. It was easily sixty pounds. I'd reeled it in while Laura slowed the boat and grabbed the net. She reached down to net the beast, and bumped the hook, freeing the fish unintentionally. I screamed a foul word as I watched it swim away. Laura looked horrified, but I wasn't cursing her. All I had wanted was a picture. The fish was a pregnant female. I would have released it anyway. She couldn't believe that I wasn't mad at her, but that's the way we were together. We simply didn't fight.

We crossed the mouth of the Chester River and rode along the banks of the Eastern Neck Wildlife Refuge. We passed Huntington Point, where G-man and I used to fish a secret rock-pile when things were slow. We weaved our way through a thousand crab pots to make the entrance to Rock Hall harbor. I chose the center channel, and tied up at the city-owned bulkhead. There were no services, but we could stay the night for free. They hold the rockfish tournament weigh-ins at this very dock, so I was familiar with it. I had always thought I'd win that tournament before I died. I'd finished in the money a few times, but never took home the big prize. Nowadays, I could care less about any fishing tournament.

Once the boat was secure, I got Laura's ashes and placed them on the table on the aft deck. Maybe she'd like to look around at our old stomping grounds while Yolanda and I got lunch. Yolanda gave me a funny look, but she didn't comment. I helped her off the boat, and we walked the few blocks to Waterman's Crab House. I ordered a dozen crabs and two beers for us. Yolanda had never eaten crabs. We spent the afternoon, piling up shells and guts and drinking beer. It was a fine distraction.

After we finished, we walked into town for ice cream at Durding's Store. It was an old fashion ice cream parlor that had been around for over a hundred years. Yolanda giggled like a little girl at all of the flavors, deciding on bubble gum. We walked back towards the harbor, eating our cones.

"Is this typical of small-town America?" she asked.

"Pretty much," I answered. "There are thousands of towns like this throughout the country."

"I like it," she said. "It's much better than Fort Lauderdale."

"It's nice, but I liked Galena better," I said.

"That is where you lived, before?" she asked.

"Yes, it's up the Sassafrass River, not far from here. I can't go there. Too many people know me. It would be dangerous."

"That is a shame," she said. "Such is the life you lead."

"It's okay," I said. "I miss my old friends, but I've moved on. This isn't my home anymore."

We checked on *Leap of Faith*, and she was fine. Laura's ashes sat where I had left them, just taking in the scenery. I heard music start up. It was coming from the Harbor Shack, and it sounded familiar. Off we went for margaritas and music. As soon as we entered the bar, I recognized the musician. Chris Sacks was strumming his guitar and singing about living life and having some fun. When he saw me, he messed up the lyrics. He recovered though, and transitioned into a song about needing a tropical recharge. It was good to see a familiar face, but it made me nervous. Who else might I bump into? We finished our drinks, exchanged pleasantries with Chris, and returned to the boat.

We hadn't discussed Baltimore all day. We'd just frittered away the time, eating and drinking and avoiding the obvious.

"Are you going to be okay, now?" I asked.

"Yes, thank you," she said. "I can do this. Spending the day in this little town has made me feel better about things. We can go tomorrow."

So it was settled. Tomorrow was the day. It wouldn't take much more than an hour to reach the Inner Harbor. I had taken my daughter there by boat once, and I had fished the shoals at the mouth of the Patapsco River many times. I looked up the marinas there, and settled on Harbor East Marina. I booked two nights in case we had any difficulty in meeting up with Yolanda's cousins. It was expensive. What the heck? I could afford it now.

We sat inside the salon that night, hiding from the mosquitoes. Yolanda gave me a stern look, followed by a lecture.

"Listen to me, Breeze," she began. "You need to settle with your past. We came all this way. You must come to terms with the law, and make yourself legal again. You have so much money. You can pay back what you took. Pay your taxes. Please, for me, put this all behind you. You have so much more to offer the world. Look what you have done just since I met you. You have proven to be a very resourceful man. You are wasting your god-given talents. You could be doing something great, instead of wasting away in some mosquito infested, mangrove swamp. I want you to turn yourself in."

"I see how it is," I said. "Use me to gain your freedom, and then you throw me to the wolves?"

I was trying to be funny, but she didn't get the humor. Cultural differences I supposed.

"Oh, Breeze," she said. "Never think such a thing. My heart will always be with you, for what you have done for me. I just know, that deep down, you want to do the right thing."

"How can you be so convinced of my honor, when I am not?" I asked. "Here's what you know about me. I only escaped Cuba because of my relationship with a cocaine dealer. I sell pot for a living, and make bootleg rum. You watched me bash a guy in the head with a hammer. Maybe I'm not the righteous man you think I am."

She pointed her finger at my chest and jabbed me a few times. Her words were tinged with a Spanish accent now.

"Now you listen to me," she commanded. "I have seen the good in you. You loved your wife. You were good to her. You have been very good to me, more good than I deserve. Andi told me nothing but good things about you. She thinks you are the best man she has ever met. I agree with her. You treat everyone fairly but yourself."

That last remark stung a little. I had tried to be noble by aiding her. It gave me a sense of purpose, just like spreading Laura's ashes had done. Was I being unfair to myself? I had never considered the idea. Was hiding from society, in my own little cove, being unfair? Was I simply punishing myself? Sure, I'd done a few good deeds, here and there. Was I truly a good person because of it? I really didn't know what to say to her. She just stood there with her hands on her hips, giving me a stern look.

"Promise me," she said.

"I promise, to give it some thought."

"You think long and hard, Meade Edwin Breeze," she said. "I have high hopes for you."

She had dropped the accent. She sounded just like Andi when she used my full name. Now, there were two women on this earth that felt they could use the name Meade.

"Let's get some rest," I said. "Tomorrow will be a big day. Good night, Yolanda."

"Good night," she said. "Say a prayer for me. I will pray for you."

I retired to my cabin to ruminate. I really wasn't sleepy, but I wanted to end the conversation. I thought about her mention of prayer. I had spoken to Laura's ashes more than I'd ever spoken to God. The only time I remember praying, was at that little chapel in Luperon. I'd never been much of a religious man. I was so relieved that day. I wanted to give thanks to someone. My fortunes had finally turned, and I needed to share my gratitude. I didn't ask for forgiveness, because I didn't feel worthy of forgiveness. I knew what I had done was wrong. No one was responsible but me. God was well aware of my sins, I supposed. Right then, I realized that God wouldn't forgive me, unless I first forgave myself.

I thought back to the Sunday school of my youth. Forgiveness was a major theme. We were all worthy of forgiveness in the eyes of God. All we had to do was ask. I also remembered my devout Christian mother whipping my ass with a switch. I wondered if she ever asked forgiveness for leaving welts on my butt. It felt silly, but I knelt on the floor in the narrow space between the bulkhead door and my bunk. I closed my eyes, and put my hands together like I'd done as a small child.

"Dear Lord, I hate to call on you after all I've done. I know I haven't lived a Godly life, but if you could watch over Yolanda as she makes her way in this world, I'd appreciate it. Don't let it spoil her. Keep her safe. Please reward her faith in you, because I'm not sure I can reward her faith in me. Maybe someday I'll be able to ask for my own forgiveness, but right now I'm spending my dime on her. Thank you, and amen."

In my dreams that night I saw *Leap of Faith*. She was half-sunk in Pelican Bay, listing badly to port. Laura held on to the starboard side stanchions, screaming for help. My view panned back. I was seeing her from behind bars. I couldn't get to my boat. I couldn't get to

Laura. I snapped out of it and padded quietly through the boat. We weren't sinking. Laura's ashes were still on the table out back. I picked her up and took her back to my bunk. I fell back asleep clutching the canister.

In the morning, Yolanda was bright and cheery. We watched the fishing boats pull out of the harbor as we drank our coffee. The smell of diesel fuel hung over the calm waters of Rock Hall. Sea gulls fought over a scrap of dead fish. The wingtips of a cow-nosed ray sliced the surface like shark fins.

"Take me to my destiny, Senor Breeze," said Yolanda. "I am packed and ready to face what may come. Did you sleep well?"

"Actually no," I said. "I had a bad dream, but don't worry, you weren't in it."

"You are just nervous about turning yourself in," she said. "As I was nervous about meeting my cousins. I dreamt that they were horribly deformed Siamese twins."

Her cousins were expecting us today, but they both worked until five. We would call them later and meet for dinner. The day was as sunny as Yolanda's disposition. She was ready. I untied the lines and we made our way out of the harbor. We ran the gauntlet of crab pots once again, and steered west towards the Patapsco River. On the northern side of the river's mouth, was Sparrows Point. Bethlehem Steel used to employ hundreds of workers, but it skeletal remains were the only reminder of better times.

We passed under 695, the Baltimore Beltway, before noon. Curtis Bay was off to port. Dundalk, which is basically one big sewage treatment plant, was to our starboard. Next the river split, at Fort McHenry. We passed the buoy that marks the spot where Francis Scott Key was inspired to write the Star Spangled Banner. Soon after, we entered the Inner Harbor. Both the Ravens and the Orioles had their own stadiums, just adjacent to the old Domino's Sugar plant and the Natty Boh brewery. The aquarium here was one of the best in the nation. The harbor was lined with attractions. It even boasted its own Hard-Rock Café. Fells Point was lined with bars, shoulder to shoulder. Marinas clogged the waterfront.

It had all been sanitized and made suitable for the tourism and convention trade. It was a façade. Just a few blocks away were the ghettos and slums. Dirty beggars worked the fringes of the safe zone. Homeless slept in doorways or over sewer grates. The water in the harbor itself was rank with smelly debris and city runoff. Trash accumulated along the seawall.

I found our slip and squeezed in between two modern yachts. *Miss Leap* looked out of place here. These other vessels were all fiberglass and chrome. They probably never left the dock. My boat was covered in stately teak. She was sturdy and proven. She was covered in salt. She had seen the Bahamas, off the beaten track. She had taken me to Cuba and the Dominican Republic. We had cruised the Keys together, countless times. These imposters didn't have her character. They were cheap plastic whores compared to her. I found the dockmaster's office and paid for the slip.

We walked up the docks and out onto Aliceanna Street. Across the way was the Oceanaire Seafood Room. I had been there many years ago with an old girlfriend. It was the most pretentious place I'd ever eaten. No entrée was less than a hundred bucks. A side of green beans was an extra fifteen dollars. White-coated attendants lurked behind you, waiting to swoop in and scoop up any crumbs that might hit the white linen tablecloth. We walked a little further up the street and settled on Fleming's Prime Steakhouse and Wine Bar instead. We took a seat at the bar to wait for her cousins.

Maria and Elena Aldama arrived with a flourish. They dropped the packages they were carrying and ran to hug Yolanda. Their voices were excited and all attention turned to the three of them laughing and squealing with delight. I was relieved that they were so excited to have Yolanda here. They treated her like royalty, asking all sorts of questions about Cuba. When the four of us were seated, I announced that I'd pick up the check, but they refused. Yolanda seemed at ease. She asked them all about their lives, their jobs, and their house. The conversation flowed between the three of them. I was the odd man out. I considered excusing myself, and then just disappearing into the night. I couldn't bring myself to do it. As much as I hated goodbyes, I owed it to Yolanda. They wanted to take her home with them that night. I sat dutifully by, while they became acquainted. The sisters were very pleasant. I was certain they'd be a big help to Yolanda. My mission was over.

We all walked to the marina together to pick up Yolanda's bags. I invited them aboard for a tour, but they weren't really interested. They were in a hurry to take Yolanda and leave. A crushing sadness came over me. Yolanda must have sensed it. She asked the girls for a few minutes of privacy.

"Do not be sad, Breeze," she said. "You have pushed me out of the nest. Now it is time for me to fly."

"I know. I'll be okay. You'll be okay," I said. "But I will miss you. In my own way, just know that I care for you, as much as I am able."

"And I will always love the great and mighty Breeze," she said. "Please remember me fondly."

She held me in a long embrace. She did not fall to the floor sobbing. I didn't drag her across the floor as she held onto my leg. She gave me a pretty smile as she let me go.

"Vaya con Dios, Breeze. I will never forget you."

She walked away. I was alone. I was alone in a god-forsaken city with no more purpose in life.

I made it through the night by drinking rum until I couldn't speak.

Vaya con Dios, Yolanda. Vaya con Dios.

After Yolanda

I had already paid for a second night at the marina, so I spent a day checking out the Inner Harbor. The aquarium was excellent, but I couldn't help but think that I could see these creatures in the wild for free. I did some afternoon bar-hopping after I found myself in Fell's Point. First stop was Max's Taphouse. They boasted of stocking over a thousand kinds of beer. I thought maybe I might try them all. That's the kind of mood I was in. I moved on to Slainte Irish Pub. The patrons were all agog over some soccer game, so I didn't stay long. I stepped into The Get Down, on Bond Street, and found DJs and an upscale party going on. I lingered long enough to see that I was the oldest person in the joint.

I walked past Ramshead Live and entered a place called Wit and Wisdom. It was a nice tavern, but seemed to be occupied by nothing but couples. I stuck my head in The Hippo. It was clearly a gay bar, so I moved on. I ended up settling on the Mt. Washington Tavern. I drank craft beers until my teeth were floating. I didn't want to walk any further. The ghettos beyond Johns Hopkins Hospital were only a block or two away.

I was just drinking for something to do. I was anonymous in this place. It felt strange walking around in the open like a normal person, but I had no direction. I really didn't know what to do with myself. I had spent a year with Andi. Together we completed a quest that had consumed me. The next year I labored in Pelican Bay, tending pot plants. I had made monthly runs to Marathon to sell my dope. It had barely provided enough money to eat and keep the boat afloat. I trudged along though, knowing that I'd someday sell that big Grand Banks and be financially secure.

Then, along came Yolanda, and a new mission. It had all worked out for the best. I had gotten my money, and fulfilled by obligation. Why didn't I feel better about it? Instead, I felt empty. I also felt a little homesick. I had dreaded each new city as we traveled from Fort Lauderdale to Baltimore. I yearned for the peace and solitude of Pelican Bay, but what was there to return to? I didn't need to grow dope now. It was just a place to be, my favorite place. It was a long trip back. I'd be alone. That thought didn't do much to improve my mood.

I decided I'd try to see my daughter. I was in no hurry. I had no other place to be. I didn't know where she lived, but I did know that she and her husband ran a restaurant. It was part of a marina, so it would be accessible by boat. The place was called Aqua Sol, and it was located just off the C & D Canal, in Summit North Marina. I'd been there by boat once, a long time ago. I'd also been there by car a few times. It was a trendy, upscale joint that served Miami style dishes and had good local musicians. I'd go in for dinner. Alison would be there, either behind the bar or in the kitchen.

Back down the Patapsco River I went. Once out into the bay, I steered east for a bit, to avoid Man-O-War Shoal. Halfway across I turned north, and aimed for the mouth of the Sassafras River. I could see the beach at Betterton. I would have loved to cruise up that scenic river and anchor behind my old home, but it was too risky. The Turkey Point lighthouse lay directly ahead. This marked the northern terminus of the bay proper. To the left was the Northeast River. To the right was the Elk River. I took the Elk past the Bohemia, and into the canal entrance.

The Chesapeake and Delaware Canal had always fascinated me. It was a man-made, deep ditch that had been dug before the advent of heavy equipment. Mules were used to pull dredges from the banks of the canal. Millions of tons of earth were moved. Its completion allowed shipping traffic to make a shortcut from northern ports like Philadelphia, to Baltimore. To this day, huge freighters traverse the narrow canal almost daily. It can make for a nervous trip if you encounter one on your way through.

Eventually, I crossed the Delaware line and found the entrance to the marina. After tying up I climbed the steep hill up to the marina office. After settling up with the dockmaster, I walked over to the restaurant.

Alison was at the bar, laughing and chatting up her customers. When she saw me, she looked shocked.

"Glad to know you're alive, Pops," she said.

"I was sort of in the neighborhood," I replied. "You can't let anyone know I'm here."

"Figures," she said with a shrug. "Can you stay a bit? See the kids?"

"I'd love to, if you'll have me," I answered.

"Of course I will," she said. "I've missed you. It's really good to see you."

Then I saw a pair of familiar faces. An old co-worker and his wife had walked in the front door and were waiting for a receptionist. Alison grabbed a couple of menus and headed their way. I heard him ask her a question.

"Is that your father? Breeze is here?"

Brown-nose Eric and I had once been friends. His office was across from mine. I knew his wife, his kids, and even his dogs. They had even dog-sat for my old hound a few times. He didn't really do much for the company, except play golf and pad his expense account. He had survived by glad-handing and saying yes, a lot. He lived in Middletown, not far from here.

I cursed my misfortune yet again. He walked toward me at the bar. I had pushed my luck too far in coming here. He was probably one of the last people I needed to be seen by.

"What are doing around here?" he asked.

"I just wanted to see my daughter, Eric," I said. "Be cool, okay?"

"I will not be cool," he said. "I'm calling the cops."

He pulled his phone from its case on his belt. He entered only three numbers.

Shit, shit, shit, Breeze. You're screwed now.

I had no choice but to run. I begged Alison for forgiveness and promised to call. I could hear Eric speaking to his phone on my way out the door.

"Yes, there's a fugitive from the law here," he was saying.

I scampered down the steps to the docks and fired up *Miss Leap*. As I pulled away, I could see my daughter standing at the top of the hill with her arms crossed. I felt like a complete ass.

At that moment, my mind was made up. I would not turn myself in. When Eric said he was calling the cops, I never once considered just standing there and letting them take me in. My first instinct was to take flight. I could go east or west, to the Delaware Bay or the Chesapeake Bay. I quickly decided on the Chesapeake. There were many more places to hide, and I was more familiar with it. Would the police martial a boat and come after me on the water? I wasn't sure I was worth the trouble.

When I reached the Elk River, I was faced with another decision. Upriver was a dead end. The Susquehanna Flats lay on the other side of Turkey Point. Havre De Grace and Port Deposit sat on opposites banks of the river. No, I'd be trapped in any of those places. I turned south, and made fast for the Sassafrass River. One mile in was a very secluded cove called Lloyd's Creek. I couldn't get in very far, because it was too shallow, but I could tuck in far enough to hide. Boats could run right by on the main river and never see me.

I approached at a slow idle. The cut was dangerously narrow, and the current roared through it. I had fished back in here many times, but that was in a much smaller boat. *Leap of Faith* had a four foot draft. She could only make it a few hundred feet inside. I got the anchor down and waited. Sunset came, but no boats appeared. I listened to the VHF for any signs of a search, but heard nothing. I knew that law enforcement had their own radio frequency, so I didn't assume I was in the clear. The night passed quietly. I held off on the rum, so I could keep my wits about me.

When I woke, it took me a few minutes to figure out where I was, and why. I was twelve hundred miles from home. Yolanda was gone. I had totally botched things with my daughter, and now the law had been alerted to my presence. No matter how hard I tried, I always seemed to end up at rock bottom. Despair was a powerful magnet and I was made out of steel. It always found me and pulled me back down.

There was nothing to do but keep running. If I could get back home, things would be alright. I had the money now. I never needed to work again. I could retire from the pot business and do some more fishing. I could afford to eat out, when I went to town. Maybe I'd find a woman someday. Maybe I'd find a woman who could stir in me the things that I missed most.

I eased out of Lloyd's Creek and into the Sassafrass. I rounded Betterton Beach and headed south. I pushed the throttle forward until we reached over seven knots of speed. We were southbound and down. With luck I'd reach the Virginia border before dark. After that I'd disappear on the ICW, just another anonymous boat heading south for the winter. I hammered south all day, looking back occasionally and eying any boats that looked like the law. I made it over eighty miles before darkness approached. I was still in Maryland waters. I anchored outside the Nanticoke River, near Bloodsworth Island. No boats approached me. There were only a few fishermen, running home before it got dark. I was a long way from Brown-nose Eric, and whatever officer that may have responded to his call.

I tried to relax. I pondered what to do with myself going forward. I was at a new stage in my life. I didn't have to crawl through the mangroves to tend to my crop. I was still a wanted man though. I'd still have to be careful. I couldn't get lazy or stupid. Any encounter with law enforcement would reveal the warrants for my arrest. I couldn't use my passport. Maybe I could buy a new identity, become a citizen of the real world that way. The more I thought about it, the more I just wanted to sit on the beach at Cayo Costa. It would be nice to have someone to share it with, but either that would come or it wouldn't. Finally, I fell asleep. I dreamt of fighting monster tarpon in the Boca Grande Pass.

The next day, I made it to Kiptopeake, on the southern tip of Virginia's eastern shore. I anchored by the concrete ships that form a breakwater for the little harbor with a boat ramp. If the weather was good, I could run down the coast on the outside, passing Virginia Beach. If it was too windy, I'd go back over to Norfolk and run down the ditch, on the inside. I broke out my fishing rod and jigged up a nice Tautog off the concrete ships. The "Tog" is not found in Florida waters, so it was a nice change of pace for dinner. While I ate, I looked over my charts. I intended to cut across the state of Florida via the Okochobee Waterway. I had never made that trip before, but I thought it prudent to avoid the Keys on my way home.

I checked the weather forecast as well. It would be a much shorter trip, if I was able to run outside, in the ocean. I could stay underway at night, avoid all the traffic and bridges, and cut the trip in half. The National Weather service was calling for light west winds over the next few days. They looked to increase on day three or four, but I could duck in somewhere and pick up the ICW again.

I thought it would be a snap. I was an offshore veteran now. I had tangled with large chunks of the Atlantic and the Caribbean. It shouldn't be a problem to run a few days off the coast. I was wrong. The winds turned to the north at the end of the second day. I was caught in a maelstrom off of Nags Head. The closest safe harbor was Oregon Inlet, but it was treacherous in rough weather. Powerful fishing boats had trouble negotiating it when the winds blew like this. My slow moving trawler wouldn't stand a chance. The near-shore waters were strewn with shoals and wrecks. I had no option but to continue south. It was still a good run to Hatteras Inlet, but I could get inside in one piece.

The north winds collided with the northerly current and caused the waves to stack up sharply. Breaking, cresting walls of ocean slammed into the bow as I plowed along. The jagged battering slowed us down to only five knots. A particularly strong gust tore a piece of canvas off the bridge enclosure. Now the rain found its way in. Salt encrusted the windshield, reducing visibility drastically. The rain washed it off, but it reformed after the next crashing wave. I didn't know if it was rain or saltwater from the sea, but a flood formed under the console. The water ran several inches deep around my feet. It sluiced off the back and created a waterfall onto the lower deck.

I had put *Miss Leap*, and myself, in danger once again, but we pulled through. Hatteras Inlet accepted us like a long lost son. It cradled us in safety and sheltered us from the storm. I secured the anchor and went to check on the damage. I apologized to my boat. I had water dripping down the wall onto the lower helm. I opened the electrical panel and was horrified at what I'd found. Water cascaded over the connections like someone was running a garden hose. Both the AC and DC power terminals were drenched. This was not good.

I climbed back up to the bridge to investigate. I shined a flashlight in the compartment under the console. The water was four inches deep. I crawled through it and located the chase that carries all the wires up to the bridge. It was under water. I couldn't see where all the water was coming from, but I had to give it a way out. I got a big screwdriver and a hammer. I wedged the screwdriver between the deck and the console and drove it in, creating a gap. Water poured out. The water level around the chase was receding. Back downstairs, the panel no longer had flowing water, but it was soaked.

I was afraid to use the inverter, or other electrical outlets. I ran an extension cord directly from the generator and plugged in a hair dryer. I'm not sure which woman had left it behind, but it would come in handy now. I spent an hour just drying out all the electrical connections. I sprayed everything down with WD-40 when I was done. When the storm was finally over, I checked out the system, and everything worked. I vowed to stay in the ICW's protected waters for the rest of the trip. *Damn you weatherman.*

Thankfully, I had no more problems with the boat, or the weather, as I made my way to Florida. The rest of the trip was tedious and boring. Day after day I motored south. Each afternoon I had to find a place to anchor or tie up for the night. The lack of company made the days last forever. I had no one to talk to. The further I went, the lonelier I felt.

It was like coming down off of a high. Apparently, I was only happy when I was off slaying dragons and rescuing fair maidens. Adventure was my drug. I tried to figure out how that came to be. I never started out seeking adventure. I had only wanted to hide from the ills of society, alone on a white sand beach. I was reasonably content to float in a quiet cove. I enjoyed the peace and serenity. I appreciated the calm beauty of nature all around me. Somewhere along the line, I had transformed. Experiencing real fear, and dancing on the edge of danger, had made me feel alive.

Having a clear goal, making a plan, and executing that plan, had made me feel worthwhile. Now there was no goal, other than going back home. There was no plan, other than wasting my life away in the sun and surf of Cayo Costa. I would go back to being an ordinary boat bum. I'd be trawler trash with secret cash this time, though. Life would be easier.

There were no real dangers to face as I traveled south on the protected waterway. The days continued to drag as I made it through North Carolina, Georgia, and finally to Florida. My spirits lifted when I crossed the border into the Sunshine State. I still had a long way to go, but there were no more state lines to cross. Instead, I'd cross the state via the Okochobee Waterway. I left the ICW at mile marker 988 and entered the St. Lucie River.

The first stretch of the river was narrow and shallow. It was also crowded with speeding boats running to and from the ocean via the St. Lucie Inlet. Then it opened up, and the long finger of Sewalls Point stretched downstream on the eastern side. The high ground was heavily wooded. Estates dotted the landscaped terrain. As I continued upriver, I navigated four bridges within the first six miles. I encountered no difficulties. I approached Stuart, and found a cluster of marinas and shore-side facilities. There were several vessels on mooring balls, so I decided to join them for the night. I took the dinghy in to Sunset Bay Marina to pay for the ball. Downtown Stuart was only three blocks east of the dock, so I set off to see what I could see. I walked past the Lyric Theater, gift shops, art galleries and trendy looking restaurants. I chose the Flagler Grill, and ate a fine steak, alone at the bar. Afterwards, I dug out an old copy of Dozier's Waterway Guide, to research the crossing to come. I had never taken this route, and wasn't properly prepared.

The next morning I reached my first obstacle at mile fifteen. The St. Lucie Lock appeared in front of me. I located a sign that read "Arrival Point," and approached it slowly. I hailed the lockmaster on channel 13. The only lock I was familiar with was a small, self-serve contraption off the Myakka River.

I had always enlisted friends to help with the lines when going through it. I had helped them negotiate it in return. Colorado Bob had bought me a sandwich and beer for my assistance. Oregon Rod brought a twelve-pack and drank most of it along the way.

"Go ahead, *Leap of Faith*," said the lockmaster. "This is the St. Lucie Lock."

"I'm single-handed," I told him. "Any help you can give me would be greatly appreciated."

"We strongly discourage passing through the locks alone," he said.

"I'm all I've got, Mack," I replied. "I'll be alright, if you can give me a hand."

"Lay her up on your starboard side nice and easy," he said. "I'll drop lines down to you, fore and aft. Have some fenders out."

I did as I was told. I held her steady, then hustled to grab the lines and tied her off.

"Now get back at the helm," he said. "When the water comes in it rushes pretty fast. If your lines get too tight, put her in gear for a minute."

"I understand," I said. "Ready when you are."

A loud buzzer sounded and the gates in front of me slowly opened. I could feel the force of the water pushing us backward. At the same time, I was going up, as the water level inside the lock increased. I watched the depth gauge that was painted on a board bolted to the seawall. We went up thirteen feet before the incoming water slowed and leveled off.

"Toss the lines and pull on out of here," said the lockmaster. "I'll pull them in after I get the gates closed."

"Thanks man," I said. "Appreciate your help."

I steered out of the lock and motored on towards Indiantown. I had no trouble with the railroad bridge there, and continued on for Mayaca. The lock here would put me into Lake Okochobee. The direct route across was another twenty-five miles to Clewiston. I'd stop near there. Lake O is the second largest freshwater lake located wholly in the continental United States, after Lake Michigan. The direct route was open water, but it was shallow. I followed the magenta line on my chartplotter closely. Four hours later I made it to the lock on the Clewiston side of the lake. I went through the same drill with another lockmaster. He was friendly and helpful, like the last one. He even warned me not to tie off tight, as I'd be going down with the water this time.

I got a little confused after locking through, so I just continued west in search of an anchorage. I couldn't find anything that looked like a decent anchorage between Clewiston and Moor Haven. The path was now wide and deep, and small boats sped by in both directions. I was tired, so I dropped anchor just off the channel on the lake side. I got in close to the bamboo and cypress along the bank, and let out a short rode.

I sat with a cold beer and watched the gators along the banks. When the sun went down, the mosquitoes came out. I closed up and called it a night. I still had more locks and bridges ahead of me, but I had the hang of it now. I was about halfway to the west coast and making good progress. I could reach Fort Myers Beach in two more days.

The Moore Haven lock dropped me into the Caloosahatchee Canal. Twenty-five more miles later, after clearing the Ortona Lock, I reached La Belle. The drawbridge had enough clearance for me to go under without opening. Just beyond the bridge, I found the free town dock that I'd heard about from several other cruisers. I tied up and walked a short distance into town. Within four blocks were a hardware store, a bank, a laundromat, a post office, a supermarket, and a tackle shop. I saw no restaurant. There was a park across the highway, but I didn't feel like crossing it. I returned to the boat and fixed my own dinner. There was some wake from passing boats, but that would quit after dark. It was only fifty more miles to Ft. Myers Beach. I'd be there the next day.

Back in SW Florida

I made good time and entered Matanzas Pass well before dark. I could easily afford a mooring ball at Fort Myers Beach, but I decided to anchor in the backwater. I wanted to see if any of my friends were still around. One-legged Beth was the first to greet me. She pulled up in her skiff with a hearty hello. She climbed aboard with a nimbleness that most people with two legs can't exhibit.

"Welcome back, Breeze," she said. "You gonna stay awhile?"

"A little bit," I said. "I wanted to check in on all of you, and I need some supplies. I'll be heading on to Pelican Bay shortly."

"Robin and Diver Dan are still here," she said. "We need to all get together and get our drink on."

"Fine by me, Beth. Bring them over tomorrow."

"We also have a new addition to the neighborhood," she told me. "You'll like her. She's a hottie."

She pointed at a big Beneteau sailboat anchored to our north. It was called *Another Adventure*.

"She came in about two months ago," said Beth. "She likes to party and she's really nice."

"She single?" I asked.

"She's on that boat by herself. We don't know what her status is otherwise."

"Thanks, Beth. I think I might want to meet her."

"If I see her, I'll invite her over tomorrow, if that's okay," she said.

"Yea, sure," I said. "Happy hour starts at five."

I hadn't laid eyes on this new woman yet, but I started to imagine what she might be like. Maybe this was just what I needed. Maybe she'd be someone who could take my mind off of the last two years, and the women I'd left behind. I was feeling hopeful. Tomorrow is a new day. I was back in familiar waters and feeling a little bit better about my prospects for a happy future. Time moves on. Andi was gone. Yolanda was gone. Most of all, Laura was gone. I had found financial freedom now. It was time to move on.

The first dinghy to arrive the next afternoon was driven by a cute, little, blond pixie. She wore a ball cap. One tuft of her hair stuck out of the hole in the back where it fastened. It wasn't long enough to be a pony tail. It just sort of puffed out of the back of her cap. She wore no makeup that I could see. She was short, and a bit stocky. Her legs were lean and muscular. Her ass was perfect. It screamed to be squeezed. Her orange shorts were tight. Her green eyes sparkled as she gave me a big smile. She introduced herself as Joy.

"That's the perfect name for you," I said. "Welcome aboard."

"Why do you say that?" she asked.

"You seem to be glowing with happiness," I answered. "Like life is a joy ride."

"To tell you the truth," she said. "It's not my given name. I needed to choose a new name, and I liked Joy."

"Nice to meet you, Joy," I said. "I'm Breeze."

"Did you make that up too?" she asked.

"It's my last name," I said. "I've been using it for almost forty years."

"Joy meets Breeze," she said. "It's got a nice ring to it."

She simply bubbled with effervescence. I was trying to think of something witty to say when the rest of the gang showed up. Robin, Diver Dan, and one-legged Beth were all piled in Dan's little dive boat. We exchanged greetings and broke out the beers. It flowed like spring water running down a mountain during the thaw. They wanted to hear all about my latest adventures. They really seemed happy to see me.

I'd forgotten what it was like to be among friends. We laughed and drank and told stories late into the night.

Whenever I looked Joy's way, she was returning my gaze. She listened intently to my tales, but also engaged the others. She herself was engaging. She had a free and easy manner about her that was attractive. She wasn't uptight at all. She didn't talk about herself though, like the rest of us did. Apparently her past was a mystery to my friends. I couldn't help but be curious, but any attempt to draw information out of her was adeptly avoided. I was intrigued.

Beth rounded up her cohorts and told them it was time to leave. I thought she might be playing matchmaker with Joy and I. When we were left alone, I asked Joy for a date.

"You want to have a drink with me tomorrow at the Upper Deck?" I asked.

"Sure," she answered. "But I have to warn you. I flirt with all the guys in there, so they'll buy me drinks. If you're uncomfortable with that, we can go someplace else. And it's not a date. It's just two friends having a drink."

"Okay," I said. "If I buy you a drink will you flirt with me?"

"I will," she said. "I will sit by you and smile pretty, until the drink is gone."

"It sounds like you have a pretty good racket going on," I said.

"That's not the half off it," she said. "A girl's got to make her way somehow. See you tomorrow."

She hopped into her dinghy and drove off towards her boat. I couldn't decide what to think of her. She was so light-hearted and carefree in appearance, but her mysterious past and that last comment belied a deeper truth. Maybe she was like me. She could be on the run from an abusive husband. She could be making her way on her wits and feminine wiles. Me, I had to sell dope, but I didn't have a gorgeous ass and beautiful smile to offer. I decided that I liked her, regardless of her untold story. I went to bed fantasizing about her, but dreamed about Laura instead.

Laura was on the other side of a bridge, over a deep ravine. A light shone around her, like an angel. As I stepped onto the bridge, it began to crumble. Laura took a step back. I stopped and watched in horror as the center span broke away and fell into the deep chasm. There was no way for me to cross. Her light faded until I could see her no more. I turned and walk away, traveling an unknown road. I kept coming to forks in the road with no guidance. I chose my directions with uncertainty, feeling lost. The dream had not ended when I awoke. I was still traveling in the wilderness, wondering which way to go.

Having drinks with Joy was a trip. She had the whole bar in the palm of her hand. The old men would giggle when she gave them some attention. The younger guys would strut their stuff, and try their best pick-up lines. She treated them all equally. They got that smile, and maybe a light touch on the arm. She got her drinks and plenty of compliments. She had time for me too, as she flitted about the place. I was happy to be a part of the show. She owned the joint, and everyone knew that she had come in with me.

She literally skipped back to the dinghy dock, singing a happy song. She was making life her playground. I had wanted to invite her back to my boat, but she hopped off the dock and fired her engine.

"Last one through the mooring field is a rotten egg," she yelled.

"No fair," I yelled back. "You got a head start."

"You snooze you lose, Breezie boy," she whooped.

She took off at full throttle across the harbor, which was a no-wake zone. There was no way I could catch her, so I obeyed the law and slowly made my way home.

I fell into a rhythm there in Fort Myers Beach. I spent my days provisioning and taking care of the boat. I spent my nights partying. Joy and I would go to town a few nights a week. Diver Dan and crew would drink with me on other nights. Some nights I was alone, but I still drank. Joy was always frantic and fun. She pointed out people to me. That guy has taken off his wedding ring, she'd say. He's looking to cheat on his wife. She'd point out a man and call him an abuser, saying she could just tell. She was very alert. She watched everyone, and made a quick judgment on their character. She knew who would buy her a drink, and who to stay away from. I bought her drinks too, of course. She was really sweet to me, but she wasn't letting me get too close.

We never got close to going to bed together, until I told her I was leaving. It was time for me to leave town, and head to Pelican Bay.

"Okay if I come to your boat and give you a little going away present?" she asked.

"I'd like that," I answered.

"How do you feel about sex with no strings attached?" she said.

"I think that it might be the best kind," I answered.

"Good answer," she laughed. "Show me what you got Mr. Breeze. Just don't go getting attached."

The sex was as playful as her attitude. There was tickling and laughter and rolling on the floor. She made me feel free and loose like her. I felt no pressure to perform great feats of sexual skill, but I gave it my best shot. When it was over, she reminded me that it was all in fun. I thanked her for the fun, and let her dress and leave without any serious conversation. The next morning she dropped by to say goodbye. I invited her to come see me in Pelican Bay, if she ever had the notion.

"I think I'd like that," she said. "But I've got a couple of scams running here that I need to finish. Give me two months. I'll come join you for a little while."

She drove off without allowing me to ask about the scams. Now I was really curious. She admitted she was up to something. Why would she tell me that, just as I was leaving? It didn't make any sense. Oh well, I thought. Maybe I'll see her again. Maybe I won't. As much as I enjoyed her company, I needed to leave town. I'd stayed too long already. I knew it was because of her. What I didn't know was if she really liked me, or if I was just another scam victim. She was so smooth and so alluring, it was hard to tell. I thought I was too smart to let her take advantage of me, but when we were naked together, she probably could have gotten anything she wanted. It was best that I moved on.

Finally Home

I hadn't come all this way to chase after some chick with dubious character and an uncertain past, even though, I myself was of dubious character and an uncertain past. I knew all too well how that could turn out. I wanted to go home. Getting to Pelican Bay was the only goal I had left to accomplish. I was homesick after all the sea miles I'd covered. Still, as I motored under the Matanzas Bridge into San Carlos Bay, I couldn't help but wonder about Joy.

She wasn't really all that pretty. She did have a pretty face, but her body was a bit stocky for my liking. Her hair was too short. She was a notorious flirt, even in my presence. What was it about her that I found so fascinating? She seemed oblivious to the worries of the world. She was constantly smiling. She floated and sparkled and beamed a radiance that made everyone around her feel happy. How did she do that? No one knew where she came from or anything about her. It was like she had disappeared from some former life and remade herself. I supposed I had done the same thing, but she had done it better. She was a really happy person. Her happiness rubbed off on the rest of us, or anyone she came into contact with.

I shrugged it off and steered towards the lighthouse at Point Ybel. I was fortunate that *Leap of Faith* could fit under the Sanibel Causeway, thus avoiding the *Miserable Mile* at the mouth of the Caloosahatchee River. I made the turn into the ICW just south of St. James City. There were no waters on Earth that were more familiar to me than these. It was a perfect Florida day with clear skies and a light breeze. I continued to cruise the blue waters off Sanibel, and then Captiva. In a few short hours I motored between Cabbage Key and Useppa Island. I could see through the southern entrance to Pelican Bay, but continued on for the northern entrance, just inside the Boca Grande Pass.

Even though I was alone, I couldn't suppress the excitement I felt to be back. I honked the horn to a few sunbathers on the sand spit as I navigated Pelican Pass. I waved to the ferry boat leaving the park service docks. I slowed to three knots and crawled through the bay until I passed Manatee Cove. I drove over the deep hole there, until the depths came up to seven foot. I dropped anchor and back down on it until I was sure it was firmly set. This was my spot in the summer months. I was far enough away from the mangroves to discourage the mosquitoes, and in open enough air to catch the afternoon sea-breeze. Finally, I was home. After all the sea miles, all the danger and distraction, and all the women, I was back where I belonged. It felt great. I had no idea what I would do with my future, but at that moment, I didn't give a shit. I wanted the world to leave me alone for awhile. I'd be more than happy not to bother the world.

I spent the first few days fishing my old spots nearby. I pulled a redfish off the edge of the mangroves on Punta Blanca Island. I took it back to the boat and filleted it while it was still alive. I put one fillet in the freezer and promptly blackened the other in a cast iron skillet. There is absolutely no better tasting fish, than one that was swimming twenty minutes ago. There is no gourmet restaurant in the world than can provide anything so fresh. The next day I hauled a big snook out from under the docks inside Manatee Cove. Again, one fillet went in the freezer. The other went into hot oil almost immediately. On the third day, I yanked a grouper up from the rocks off the old Quarantine Docks. I was eating like a king and filling the freezer at the same time.

Then I decided to work on my tan. I went to the beach every day for weeks. I'd read for a while, then lie on a beach towel and bask in the sun. When I was sure no one was around, I'd drop the swim trunks and try to erase the white places. Each afternoon, I'd return to the boat, rinse down with fresh water, and crack open a beer. I'd sit and watch the sun go down in complete silence. I only had my thoughts to keep me company. For a long time, that was enough. I reconciled my relationship with Andi. I allowed myself to be proud for rescuing Yolanda. I told myself it was okay that I'd left Joy behind in Fort Myers Beach.

I'd experienced enough adventure for a lifetime. I thought I could just stay here forever, fishing and sunning on the beach. Let the crazy world spin on without me. I needed that time, and it was good for me. It was just what I needed. I slowed way down, and let myself be lazy. Most folks can't stand to be alone. They can't tolerate the silence, or their own thoughts. They constantly seek distraction. I learned to live without all the noise that comes with everyday society. Instead I looked forward to the breath of dolphins each morning. I tried to identify the ospreys by the sharp trill of their calls. I recognized the manatees by the pattern of prop scars on their backs. I could judge the wind speed by the sound of wavelets lapping at my hull. Time was of no essence. There was daytime, and nighttime. There was sunrise, and sunset. I had the morning calm, and the afternoon sea breeze. I had the tides, the moon phase, and a million stars in the Milky Way.

I let life pass me by for almost two months. Fishing was good. The beer was cold. My skin was a deep brown. I gained a few pounds and it helped erase some of the wrinkles around my eyes. I felt healthy, and stronger. I also felt a subtle change in the wind. Instead of lying on the beach, I started walking. The walks got longer and sometimes turned into jogs. I started to find myself burning off energy by thinking up new boat chores. I rose earlier each morning. I was getting restless.

I didn't really care to be restless, but there it was. There was no denying it. The restorative powers of peace had made me whole again. Now my soul was searching for something to do. I came to terms with it, but at first, I couldn't figure out what to do about it. I had no goals in life. There were no dragons to slay, nor fair maidens to rescue. I thought I'd probably had my fill of glorious quests. I pondered my dilemma for days. I was a blank slate. I could do anything, or go anywhere. I was free, but I was alone. I hadn't talked to another living person in almost two months. I didn't mind the solitude. In fact, I rather enjoyed it. Something was bubbling underneath the surface, though. I was developing an itch that would need to be scratched.

Eventually, an idea presented itself. I was walking the interior of Cayo Costa when I stumbled upon one of my old markers. I'd left small signs to indicate where my hidden pot plants were. I put a pointed stick in the ground, or lined three rocks in a row, to indicate the entrance in the underbrush. The narrow tunnel was almost completely overgrown now. I got down and crawled through the sea grapes and scrub until I came to a small clearing. This particular plant had grown quite full and tall until falling over from its own weight and apparent lack of water. It wasn't completely dry and brown. It still had some green to it, and lots of buds. It would yield a good half-pound of quality product. Operation Island Smile could be back in business.

I didn't need the money, but it would give me something to do. I spent a few days checking on the other plants. I never did find them all. Some had died long ago and were worthless. Some had thrived in my absence. Over the next few days, I harvested what I could salvage. I kept an eye out for rangers, and the unpredictable helicopters that sprayed insecticides. I crawled around the cactus. I trimmed back the tunnels. I picked the ripe sea grapes for snacks, and washed them down with bottled water. When I was done, I had roughly two pounds of dope ready for market.

It would be just like the old days. I'd motor down the coast, across Florida Bay, and into Boot Key Harbor. I'd see the gang at Dockside, and sell my wares to Tiki Terry. If it all went well, maybe I'd plant a new crop, stay in the farming business. Maybe I could even dig up the old rum still and cook up a few batches. Just because I had money now, didn't mean I couldn't still be a pirate. Law be damned. I lived outside the law. That was my place in the world now, and I was damned good at it.

I'd run dope and cocaine in the Florida Keys. I'd escaped an agent by jumping in my dinghy. I'd talked my way out of a Cuban jail. I'd bested the henchmen of a kingpin. I'd brought back a load of cash all the way from the Dominican Republic. I'd navigated the Bahamas beneath the radar, never showing a passport; twice. I'd escaped the cops and an ex-coworker on the Chesapeake Bay. I'd left one pretty girl in Luperon, and another in Baltimore. The storms couldn't stop me either. I'd taken the worst that man or the sea could throw at me, yet here I was alive and well. A quick trip down the coast with a few pounds of pot would be child's play for me and my mighty vessel. There was nothing to it, yet the prospect made me feel alive.

I reversed my path on the ICW and headed south towards Sanibel. Dolphins played in my bow wake inside Captiva Pass. Cormorants shared space on the channel markers with pelicans. The air was salty, with a touch of diesel. I loved being underway aboard *Leap of Faith*. I was so comfortable at the helm, feeling her rhythm. We were one on days like this. I felt that I had been born to captain a boat in these waters. Everywhere else was foreign territory, but I owned this coastal stretch of southwest Florida.

Just as I was about to leave the ICW on the south end of Sanibel, I saw a big Beneteau coming down from the Caloosahatchee, with the sails up. It was rare to see sails flying here. It took a true sailor to navigate the narrow channels without the engine. I slowed to allow it to get closer before I turned. Sure enough, it was *Another Adventure*, with Joy at the helm. She was headed north, towards Pelican Bay.

"Another Adventure, Another Adventure, this is Leap of Faith on channel sixteen," I hailed.

"What the hell, Breeze?" she asked. "Where you going?"

"Let's go to channel sixty-eight," I answered.

"Another Adventure on sixty-eight."

"Are you heading where I think you're heading," I asked.

"I was coming to see you, Breeze," Joy answered. "What's the deal?"

"Sorry, but I've got my own scam working. I'll be back in a week, weather permitting."

"I've got a mind to turn around, Breeze," she said. "But I think I burnt one too many bridges in Fort Myers Beach."

"I'd love to hear all about it," I said. "Make yourself at home until I get back."

"What am I supposed to do all by myself?" she said. "I hear it's wilderness."

"Relax. Lay on the beach," I said. "Read a book or something. It's peaceful there. No one can find you. You'll be safe."

"Okay, Breeze," she said. "I'll try, but if I get antsy I'm moving on. I'd like to see you though."

"I'd like to see you too, Joy," I said. "Sit tight for a week, ten days tops."

"See you soon, Breezie Boy," she said. "Another Adventure back to sixteen."

"Adios, amiga," I called. "Leap of Faith back to sixteen."

That changed things significantly. I'd have something to look forward to upon my return. I could have just turned around and went back with her, but I really wanted to make this trip. A pirate wouldn't change his plans for a woman, would he? No, he wouldn't. I would do this thing. If she was waiting for me when I got back, well, that would be fine.

I shuffled Joy to the back of my mind and returned to my courtship with *Miss Leap*. Her engine purred. The rudder responded to my hands on the wheel like a woman responds to her lovers touch. I guided her gently under the causeway and out into the Gulf. We cleared the last marker and turned south for Marco. It was an easy trip under calm conditions. Normally, I would have anchored in Factory Bay. It was an easy in and out. This time, however, I turned into Collier's Creek and made my way into Smokehouse Bay. I noticed some pretty severe shoaling on the west side of the creek. I had to come within a foot or so of some fancy yachts tied to the docks on the eastern side. If that got much worse, the creek would be impassable for deep draft vessels.

I needed some supplies, food mostly. There was a grocery store in the back of Smokehouse Bay with a convenient dock just for people like me. I'd load up, spend the night, and then I'd take off at first light. Getting groceries without a car was a pain in the ass in Marathon. I made two trips and put enough food on board to last a month or more.

The next morning I departed for the mouth of Little Shark River. It took ten hours to make the approach. The winds were light out of the east, so I anchored in ten foot of water, well outside the river's entrance. It was an eerie feeling being anchored in the Gulf. I'd done it before, but it was hard to get used to. I'd seen my first green flash anchored out here. It was a mystical experience that I'll never forget. A person couldn't be more alone here. The Ten Thousand Islands and the Everglades held no human life. It was like you were the last living person on Earth.

I sat alone as the sun sank into the sea. I observed keenly, hoping for another green flash. It didn't happen. Instead, an explosion of red beamed out of the sea. It shot up into the thin clouds and burned holes in the sky. It was a deep crimson. Its reflection turned the sea to blood. It was violent, and foreboding. I'd never seen anything quite like it. It quickly softened to orange and pink. The sky became so lovely and peaceful I began to doubt that it had ever happened. Was there such a thing as a red flash? I knew that "red sky at night" meant "sailors delight", but this was something different. I wondered if anyone else on the planet had seen it the way I had. Did it do the same thing in the Keys, or on Charlotte Harbor? If not, I could have been the only living soul to see it from my lonely perch on the back deck of my boat. As I closed up for the night to keep the mosquitoes at bay, I couldn't help but feel that it was some kind of warning. I washed away the feeling of dread with an ample glass full of rum.

I took off at first light for Marathon, and Boot Key Harbor. The Gulf was like an inland lake to me now. I marveled at how far I'd come as the captain of my vessel. I'd survived huge waves in the Atlantic Ocean. I'd ridden out a hurricane in a forbidden land. I'd navigated tricky reefs in the Caribbean. I'd traveled thousands of miles over open oceans. With some skill and a lot of luck, I'd managed to not only survive, but to thrive. This was my element. For me it meant freedom and control of my own destiny. Those old pirates were on to something.

The Seven Mile Bridge welcomes cruising vessels to the Keys. I admired its architecture as I passed under the sixty-five foot high center span. The water turns very clear here. The Gulf mixes with the ocean and creates an expanse of blue that is a wonder to behold. I turned into the entrance to Boot Key Harbor, passing Pancho's and Burdines. I went through the bridge to nowhere, and entered the mooring field. Instead of calling for a mooring ball, I decided to anchor in Sister Creek. I didn't require the services provided by Marathon City Marina, and anchoring was free. I still hadn't lost all of my penny pinching habits. Anchoring in the creek requires tying stern lines off to the mangroves. This can be a tricky chore for a single-hander, but as I backed up towards the shoreline, a fellow boater came out to assist me. Besides my radio conversation with Joy, he was the first person I'd talked to in two months.

I couldn't wait to get over to Dockside and find Tiki Terry. If he wasn't there that night, he'd be in soon. Dockside was the center of all activity in the harbor, and Terry kept his finger on the pulse of Marathon. I entered the bar and looked around. Lisa wasn't behind the bar or waiting tables. When I asked about her I was told she didn't work here anymore. Later I'd see that her boat wasn't on its usual mooring. I guessed that she'd moved on. I didn't recognize any of the staff, but this place always did have a lot of turnover. None of the new crop attracted my attention. I remembered when Carol worked here. She had definitely gotten my motor running, but she was married.

I sat and nursed a few beers before Terry arrived. When he saw me, he looked alarmed. He came towards me waving his hands and shaking his head; no, no, no.

"You have got to get out of here right now, Breeze," he said. "I mean right this minute. Wherever the boat is, pull up and leave as fast as you can."

"What's going on Terry?" I asked. "I brought you some weed. Good stuff too."

"I can't buy your weed," he said. "I can't even talk to you. Get out of here, now."

"Shit, man," I said. "Some greeting."

He grabbed me by the arm and forcefully directed me out towards the dinghy dock.

"Look man," he started. "A while after you left here the last time, Bald Mark came to see me. He roughed me up pretty good. He busted some ribs. He put a pistol in my mouth. I told you not to cross that dude, Breeze. I fucking warned you. He's put word on the street that he wants you dead. I'm supposed to be on the phone with him right now. I'm supposed to call him the minute I lay eyes on you. If he finds out you were here with me, I'm dead too. Whatever you did to him, he won't let it pass. In the meantime, I'm out of business here. Bald Mark owns all the trade now, even pot. He's stronger and meaner than ever down here. Run like hell, Breeze. Never come back."

Honestly, I'd forgotten all about Bald Mark. It seemed like decades ago. My brain didn't want to recall his black eyes or his violent threats. I never wanted to remember how it felt to smash Enrique's skull either. I'd utilized selective memory quite well, but that trick wouldn't work anymore. I'd blindly stumbled into the last place on earth I needed to be. *Stupid Breeze.*

"Jesus, Terry," I said. "I'm so sorry. Shit just went down the wrong way. I never meant you any harm."

"I heard some things," he said. "You did what you had to do, but we are not friends now. I don't know you. I don't know where you are. I've never seen you here. Go."

"I understand," I said. "I'm leaving right now."

He pulled me in close and whispered to me.

"T Roy moved up to Punta Gorda," he said softly. "Take your dope to him."

"Thanks, man," I said. "I gotta go."

Just hearing the name Bald Mark, sent chills down my spine. It was a swift kick in the ass, and a hard dose of reality. The Keys were now off-limits for me. I should have known. A bad man wanted me dead. How could I have been dumb enough to walk right into his backyard? I didn't even need the money. It was just something to do. I'd let myself become soft while convalescing in Pelican Bay. I'd lost my edge. My keen ability to always be extra aware of my situation had diminished. This pirate thing was tougher than I'd thought.

My heart-rate increased as I made my way through the moored boats and into Sister Creek. I'd burned seven hours of daylight getting here. I used up a few more hours at the bar. I couldn't get far before dark, but I had to run. There was nothing else to do. I dreaded crossing Florida Bay in the dark. The sheer number of lobster pots almost guaranteed I'd catch one with the prop. I needed to hide for the night, but where? If there was anyone at Dockside that would get word to Bald Mark, he'd be looking for me immediately. Bahia Honda was close, but too obvious. Newfound Harbor was out. Boats anchored there could be seen from the highway. The last thing he would think I would do, is move north, closer to Tavernier and his marina. I decided to go back under the Seven Mile Bridge, turn north, and look for a spot to hole up in. I found it off Longpoint Key. There was only one house in sight. It was a giant mansion way out on the point. I couldn't see the highway or any other structures. There were no other boats in the area. It would have to do. I'd leave before sunup, as soon as I could see well enough to dodge the lobster pots.

I brought Laura's ashes out for the sunset. I didn't speak to her. I hadn't spoken to her in a long time. I just held her in my hand. It comforted me somewhat. Yesterday, I was the master of my domain. Today, I was on the run once again. I hoped I hadn't tempted fate one too many times. I would run, like I had always done. Was I destined to run forever?

I barely slept. I turned every sound into a boat approaching. Motorcycles passing on US1 sounded like the deep growl of Bald Mark's go-fast boats. If it was too quiet, it meant someone was sneaking up in a rowboat. I was driving myself nuts with paranoia. I couldn't wait for morning to come. When it did, I was off for home at top speed. I urged on *Miss Leap* like a jockey coaxes his mount. She pushed water out of her way with a sense of urgency. We plowed hard up beyond Cape Sable and continued on. I started to see stone crab traps off the Ten Thousand Islands, so I scanned the charts for a place to pull in for the night. I chose a stretch of deep water between Panther Key and Hog Key, well south of Goodland. I battled the bugs for a couple hours while swilling beer. I switched to rum before going to bed, and slept much better.

In the morning, I called on my vessel once again to push hard on a northward course. I skipped right on by Marco Island and made San Carlos Bay before nightfall. Instead of going into Fort Myers Beach, I continued north and anchored off St. James City. I was almost home. I remembered that Joy might be there waiting for me. I was early in my return. She should still be there. Who knew what lie ahead with me and that one? It would be good to see her again though. I'd put enough miles behind me to settle down some. Being on familiar waters calmed my nerves tremendously. I even had a friendly face to look forward to. I began to think that I'd escaped Bald Mark. I'd never once told anyone where I grew my crops. I'd even kept my hideout a secret from Tiki Terry. Only the gang at Fort Myers Beach knew where I stayed. One of them was there now, hopefully.

I contemplated how many times I'd been running from someone, without even knowing if they were chasing me. The whole concept of running in a slow-moving trawler amused me, but it always seemed to work out for me. I'd spent the past several years trying to put distance between me and whatever trouble pursued me. Somehow, I'd managed to survive, and I always ended up back in Pelican Bay. It was my safe haven in a world full of storms.

The rest of the trip was easy. I lost count of the dolphins that greeted me between Captiva and Cabbage Key. As I came alongside Useppa, I could see into the southern portion of the bay. Joy's sailboat was anchored near where I usually dropped the hook. Instead of going up toward the Pass and using the northern entrance to Pelican Bay, I decided to sneak around the southern end of Punta Blanca and anchor in the hurricane hole there. Once inside, my boat couldn't be seen unless one came into the anchorage. Sailboats with tall masts could be spotted, but not my trawler. I secured the boat, and put the dinghy down to go say hello to Joy.

She wasn't on her boat. I found her on the sand spit surrounded by a trio of young guys. She wore an orange bikini and the ever-present ball cap. She was telling them a wild sailing story using detailed hand motions and body language. They were eating it up. As I beached the dinghy, she stopped long enough to pull two beers out of their cooler. She handed me one.

"Well if it ain't the prodigal son," she said. "Didn't see you pull in."

"I'm down in the hurricane hole," I told her. "Good to see you, Joy."

"Good to see you too, Breeze," she said. "Bugs are gonna eat you alive in there."

"Bugs are the least of my worries," I said. "Tell you about it later."

She introduced me to her friends for the day. She'd been trading stories for beer all afternoon. The fact that her bikini bottom barely covered her ass may have helped some as well. I just let her do her thing. She fed me another beer whenever she got one. The guys didn't seem to notice or care. She told me she'd been doing this almost every day. She just waited until the beach filled with boats, then she came and crashed someone else's party. She had a gift for social interaction that I didn't have. I much preferred one-on-one situations.

I got a lot of that with Joy over the next few months. I showed her how to get to the private beach and she loved it. We'd sit and talk for hours, just soaking up the sun. At first it was me doing all the talking. Little by little, she coaxed my life story out of me. As I grew more comfortable with her, I told her more and more. Eventually, she'd heard all of it.

"Damn, Breeze," she said. "You've lived one badass adventure after another. I knew there was something different about you. You've seen a lot of shit."

"It's not how I planned things, believe me," I said. "But I guess I wouldn't change a thing."

"So what's the future hold for El Breezo the pirate?" she asked.

"The immediate future has you telling me your story," I answered. "Fair is fair."

"I started a new life," she began. "And since then I haven't told anyone about my old one. It's past history, like it never happened. I can barely remember the person I used to be."

"You and I have become friends, right?" I said. "Like real buddies. We hardly even have sex together, except when we're both a certain kind of drunk. I haven't had a real friend in a long time. With women, there is always tension. With men, there is always rivalry. You and I are just easy together."

"I feel it too," she said. "You don't get all jealous like every man I ever knew. You let me be me."

"Now I'm going to let you tell me your story," I said.

She took a deep breath and began to talk. She stared out at the Gulf while she spoke. She had been married, and her husband was abusive. That much I could have guessed, but this guy was a special kind of abusive. He thought *Fifty Shades of Grey* was a manual for a happy marriage. It had started out with a little light bondage. It developed into a violent, sadistic routine of sexual torture. She had objected somewhere along the way, but it didn't stop him. She was torn between her beautiful home, fancy car, high social standing, and being a slave to a sadist. His administrations grew kinkier and more painful. He couldn't get enough of her pain. His weird sexual appetites only worsened until she couldn't take it any longer.

"I drugged that sick motherfucker," she said. "I wanted to kill him. I put a pillow over his face and tried to smother him, but I couldn't do it. Instead, I took his wallet. I withdrew all the money from our accounts that

I could, and I ran away. I bought that boat and renamed myself Joy. I made it to the Keys and lived it up for a year, but that got old. All the freaks and fairies down there got on my nerves. That's how I ended up in Fort Myers Beach. Then I met you, and that's how I ended up here. It seems so long ago, Breeze. This place is so awesome. Thanks."

"Thanks for inviting you here?" I asked. "Or thanks for listening?"

"Both, I guess," she said. "Thanks for being my friend, and not some possessive asshole."

"I am the master of not being possessive," I said. "I let pretty girls be, wherever I roam. Girls I failed to possess are scattered about the globe."

"Is it because of your wife?" she asked.

"I don't know," I answered. "I'm starting to come to terms with that. I did sleep with you a couple of times, remember?"

"About that," she said. "Do you think we should, like, be a couple? Or should we abstain from sex in order to preserve our friendship?"

"I think we should leave things just the way they are, Joy," I said. "No sense ruining a good thing. Don't over-think it. Just be."

"I like that," she said. "Just be. I like that just fine."

The Reckoning

We played together for weeks. There on those islands, she was like a little girl, and I was a little boy. We found a Frisbee floating on the Gulf side and tossed it for hours. We built sandcastles and decorated our forts with shells. We played putt-putt on the sand, using a scrub brush for a gulf club. There was no more talk of our sad pasts. We visited the manatees regularly. We continued to crash parties on the sand spit. For the most part, we slept on our own boats. Occasionally, the right combination of sun and alcohol would create a sleepover. Neither of us took it too seriously, and all was right with our world.

It would all come crashing down, like waves erasing our cities of sand. I heard them coming long before I saw them. I had relocated to the larger anchorage to avoid the bugs. The deep growl of high-performance engines barked in the still air. A big Donzi with two men aboard violated the no-wake zone entering the bay. The go-fast boat was doing just that, going fast and heading my way. I just stood there at first, wondering what jerk was disturbing my peace. The coming danger didn't dawn on me, until I saw his face.

It was Enrique. That mean bastard had survived. I stood petrified with shock, which was a huge mistake. I watched as Bald Mark's main henchman bolstered himself against the coaming and raised a rifle. The driver accelerated and the increased engine noise snapped me out of my stupor. I dove to the floor of the salon at the last second. Automatic weapons fire rang out and bullets sprayed the cabin walls and windows. I crawled down the companionway and huddled between the port side bunk and the head. The storage space under the bunk was filled with recently purchased canned goods. I had a faint hope that they'd stop or slow the bullets.

The shooting stopped and I could hear the intruding boat turn to make another pass. His speed carried him in a wide arc away from me. I snatched the remote mic from the lower helm and began to scream over the VHF.

"Mayday, Mayday, Mayday. Automatic weapons fire, south end of Pelican Bay. I'm being fired on. Mayday, Mayday, Mayday. Any law enforcement in the area please respond."

"Vessel hailing Mayday, please state the nature of your emergency. This is Coast Guard Sector Saint Petersburg."

"Some idiots are shooting up my boat," I answered. "Unless you've got a boat in the area, get the FWC or the Sherriff's Department here fast."

The Coast Guard was rarely evident in these waters. The FWC and the Lee County Sherriff were here often. I hoped that one of them was nearby. As I fumbled in a locker for my shotgun, I heard the Coast Guard hailing local law enforcement. There was an FWC boat in the Boca Grande Pass, five minutes away.

A Sherriff's boat called in from the Captiva Pass, ten minutes to the south.

I pulled my 20 gauge out of the plastic trash bag I stored it in. It hadn't been fired in years. I knew that it was loaded. I just couldn't remember what shells I'd loaded it with. It was slick with gun oil, and not rusted. I crawled on the floor towards the aft door as more bullets ripped through *Miss Leap*. Holes appeared in the refrigerator and plexi-glass splintered above me. The roar of the engines was impossibly loud. Just as the demon vessel came even with my stern, I poked my head out and raised the barrel towards it. Enrique leaned down to load another clip. I could see a bald spot on the top of his head. It was shaped exactly like the head of my hammer, which now rested on the bottom of Hawk Channel, just below Rodriguez Key.

I tried to steady my weapon, and squeezed the trigger. I could tell it was bird shot by the softness of the recoil. I missed Enrique entirely, but struck the driver squarely in the upper back, nape, and back of his head. Dozens of little blood splotches sprouted out of him. The force of the shot slammed him into the wheel.

It probably wouldn't kill him, but it certainly ruined his day. The fast boat screamed off to port in another wide circle. I had some slugs for my shotgun in a drawer under the nav station. Did I have time to trade birdshot for some man-stoppers?

I looked through the shattered side windows to see Enrique dragging his wounded cohort from the helm so he could take the wheel. I turned to the aft door and spotted an FWC boat coming in from the Pass at a high rate of speed. I hoped that they wouldn't get shot up on my account. It looked like Enrique would come around for another shot at me, so I decided not to reload. Instead, I hunkered down below and hoped I wouldn't be hit. Let the law see him firing on my boat, and hope for the best. I vaguely became aware of the radio chatter. A Sherriff's boat was minutes away. A Coast Guard fast boat was enroute from offshore. It all boiled down to a few seconds. Either Enrique's bullets would find their mark, or they wouldn't. Help was very close. He had one last chance to exact his revenge.

I made myself as small as possible, tucked in behind the canned goods. I could see Laura's ashes sitting undisturbed on the nightstand. I closed my eyes as tightly as I could and braced myself for impact. The engine noise got closer. Time stood still. I could feel her presence. I could almost hear her speak to me. I could see her face in the darkness behind my eyelids. Was I going to join her?

My moment of grace was ripped apart by bullets shredding through fiberglass. Corn and peas exploded under the bunk. Laura's canister took a direct hit. A cloud of ashes blew from the nightstand and into the hall. The bullet that I was sure would rip through my flesh never came. I was covered in vegetable juice, sweat and ashes when the shooting stopped. Police boats were converging on the scene. I watched with some amusement as Enrique steered his boat towards the south and tried to run.

He knew he was faster by far, but he didn't know these waters. The southern end of Pelican Bay is one vast grass flat, less than a foot deep. I'd watched rental boats run aground on those flats a hundred times.

He was running at full speed when the bottom reached up and grabbed the lower units of his outdrives and slammed him to a stop. He flew over the windshield, out over the bow, and into the shallow water with a sickening thud. His day was done. I was still alive. Various officers descended on him. He didn't appear to be hurt too badly, but he didn't resist. I assumed his partner was still in the boat.

The lawmen began to make order out of the chaos and I pulled myself together. I wish I could tell you how brave I was throughout that day, but it just wouldn't be true. I was grateful that I hadn't shit my pants. Once my heart rate slowed, I realized that I was in deep shit. My boat was full of holes and I was literally surrounded by officers from at least three different agencies. There would be no talking myself out of this one.

Soon enough, they came to interrogate me. They needed my name and pertinent information for their reports. It wasn't long before they discovered the warrants for my arrest. A deputy with the Lee County Sherriff's Department took the lead.

"I realize you've have a traumatic day, Mr. Breeze," he began. "But we can't ignore these warrants. We know who those guys are too. They weren't shooting at you for kicks. We also have to assume you're involved in the drug trade."

That's when I remembered the dope. It was still onboard, stashed in the hold below. I'd go up on embezzlement, tax evasion, and possession with intent to deliver. I was royally fucked. I was about to put my hands out to accept the cuffs when Joy pulled up in her dinghy. The officers tried to run her off, but she was having none of it.

"Oh Breeze," she shouted. "I was sure you were dead. Thank God."

"I managed to survive again," I said. "But it looks like I'm going to jail."

"No, no, no," she cried. "You can't leave me now. Do something."

"There's nothing left to do, Joy," I said. "It's time to face the music. I'm going to pay for my sins after all. My running days are over."

Then she shocked me by climbing over the rail and wrapping me up in a tight bear hug. She bawled her eyes out. The law men stood by and let her cry. I wrapped my arms around her and rocked her gently. I thought of Laura. I thought of Andi. I thought of Yolanda. All of them were gone. In this life changing moment there was Joy. It was all coming to an end. None of it mattered anymore. There was nothing left for me, but Joy.

Epilogue

The officers were really nice. The white-collar crap didn't bother them. The dope got their attention though. Joy endeared herself to all of them and bought me some time. They let me gather my things, including my cash. I gave Joy a big wad of hundred dollars bills and instructed her to take *Leap of Faith* to Laishley Park Marina in Punta Gorda. I told her to look for Oregon Rod, on A-Dock. He would help however he could, and bring her back to her boat.

The arrest was made by Lee County officers, so they took me to Fort Myers. I would await extradition to Delaware in the county detention center. Before the Delaware authorities came for me, Joy paid a visit.

She promised to wait for me.

The End

If you enjoyed this book, please leave a review at Amazon. Thank you.

Acknowledgments

Interior formatting by http://ebooklaunch.com/

Cover design by http://ebooklaunch.com/

Cover photo by Ed Robinson

Other Books by Ed Robinson

Leap of Faith; Quit Your Job and Live on a Boat

Poop, Booze, and Bikinis

The Untold Story of Kim

Trawler Trash; Confessions of a Boat Bum

Visit Ed's blog at
http://quityourjobandliveonaboat.com/

Connect on Facebook at
www.facebook.com/quityourjobandliveonaboat

Email Ed at
kimandedrobinson@gmail.com

Made in the USA
Monee, IL
12 September 2020

42279549R00164